Becoming Who You Are

Becoming Who You Are

Insights on the True Self from Thomas Merton and Other Saints

James Martin, SJ

HiddenSpring

Imprimi potest: Very Rev. Thomas J. Regan, SJ,
Provincial, Society of Jesus of New England.

May 10, 2005, Boston, Massachusetts

The Scripture quotations contained herein are from the New Revised Standard Version: Catholic Edition © 1989 and 1993, by the Division of Christian Education of the National Council of the Churches of Christ in the United States of America. Used by permission. All rights reserved.

Cover by Stefan Killen Design
Book design by Lynn Else

Library of Congress Cataloging-in-Publication Data

Martin James, SJ
    Becoming who you are : insights on the true self from Thomas Merton and other saints / James Martin, SJ.
        p. cm.
    Includes bibliographical references.
    ISBN 1-58768-036-X (alk. paper)
    1. Self—Religious aspects—Christianity. 2. Theological anthropology. 3. Merton, Thomas, 1915-1968. I. Title.
    BT713.M37 2006
    248—dc22

                                                        2006007983

Published by
HiddenSpring
an imprint of Paulist Press
997 Macarthur Boulevard
Mahwah, New Jersey 07430

www.hiddenspringbooks.com

Printed and bound in the United States of America

Contents

Dedicated to
David I. Donovan, SJ
1940–2005
A wise spiritual director, faithful priest, and generous friend
who helped me to become who I am.

Introduction

For me to be a saint means to be myself," wrote the Trappist monk Thomas Merton in his book *New Seeds of Contemplation*. "Therefore the problem of sanctity and salvation is in fact the problem of finding out who I am and discovering my true self."

There are few lines in contemporary spirituality more powerful than those. One could spend a lifetime pondering and putting into effect that insight.

Of course the same idea has been said elsewhere, many times and in many ways, from philosophers to saints to ecumenical councils. But somehow Merton's descriptions of what it means to be your "true self" and the temptations of trying to be the "false self" (more about that later) have been the most meaningful to me. Perhaps that's because Merton himself has been so meaningful in my life. (More about that later, too.)

This short book is a meditation based on Thomas Merton's idea of the true self. It grew out of a lecture given at Corpus Christi Church in New York City in 2005. Every year, the church sponsors an afternoon lecture celebrating the lives of Thomas Merton and another popular author, Henri Nouwen, the Dutch priest whose own writings on the spiritual life, like Merton's, have influenced many readers.

In a nice touch, the annual lecture is held sometime around the end of January, as a way of commemorating the nearby birthdays of the two men: Merton was born on January 31, 1915, and Nouwen on January 24, 1932. The lecture is also sponsored by the Catholic archdiocese of New York and the Henri Nouwen Center, an international organization whose goal is to introduce the public to Nouwen's life and writings.

Corpus Christi Church was an important place in Thomas Merton's life, a fact that may not be familiar to all readers. So a short biography may be in order.

Chapter One

The Short Life of Thomas Merton

T homas Merton was born in 1915, in a small French town called Prades. His mother, Ruth, was an American artist and dancer. Owen, his father, was a New Zealander and a painter of some renown. "My father painted like Cézanne," wrote Merton with evident pride. In 1918, after the tight-knit family had moved to New York to be nearer to Ruth's parents, another son, John Paul, was born.

When Tom was almost six, his mother died after a battle with stomach cancer. Immediately afterward, Tom and his brother were left with their grandparents in New York while their restless father traveled and painted. Owen returned after a year, and brought his eldest son to live with him, first in Bermuda and then in France. During this period, Tom was often sent to board with a variety of his father's acquaintances, friends and relatives.

One family with whom Tom stayed was the Privats, staunch Catholics whose simple piety made a lasting impression on the young boy. (Merton's father was not an especially religious man.) In one of the most touching passages in his autobiography *The Seven Storey Mountain*, Merton wonders how much of his later life was owed to their example. He writes, "But one day I shall know, and it is good to be able to be confident that I will see them again and be able to thank them."

Tom was educated first in France in a local *lycée* and then at an English boarding school called Oakham, and finally at Clare College, University of Cambridge. When he was sixteen, and still at Oakham, his father died from cancer. Perhaps because of the early deaths of both parents, his moving from one house and country to another, and his rootless existence, Tom's childhood was a sad one by all accounts. He entered Cambridge as a bright, well-traveled, but rather lonely young man.

While still a student at Cambridge, Tom fathered a child. It is a hazy incident that was concealed in some pious biographies of Merton, and, according to at least one source, was later removed from his autobiography by his religious superiors in the Trappist order. According to some biographers, the woman and the child were killed in the German air raids on England during the Second World War. Later attempts to locate them came to naught.

Not long after Owen's death, Tom's godfather and guardian, Dr. Tom Bennett, suggested that he complete his education at Columbia University in New York. Tom readily agreed, having found neither Oakham nor Cambridge to his liking. He had also lost his scholarship at Cambridge due to a combination of bad grades, drinking and general carousing.

Tom began his studies at Columbia in 1935. While there, he met a group of young men who would remain his pals for the rest of his life. He both wrote and drew a bit for the campus humor magazine, *The Jester*, continued to drink a good deal, and eventually received his undergraduate degree. He also, gradually, became more interested in religion. Raised a desultory Christian, Merton found himself attracted to Catholicism through a variety of sources: through his intellect, through art, through his emotional life, and through the example of the few other Catholics he knew. One day, sitting in his room reading about the Jesuit poet Gerard Manley Hopkins, Merton decided that he wanted to be baptized a Catholic. "What are you waiting for?" a voice within him seemed to say.

In November of 1938, to the astonishment of his friends, who knew him as more a carouser than anything else, Tom was baptized at Corpus Christi Church. The white marble font is still there, very near the entrance to the church.

After his conversion to Catholicism, Tom's life changed rapidly. He finished his master's degree in English at Columbia and almost immediately began to consider becoming a priest. With the enthusiastic zeal of the convert, Tom approached the Franciscans about entering their order, but was rejected, most likely because he had fathered a child. (Other sources suggest that Merton was viewed by the Franciscans more as a solitary fellow than a community-minded man, which counted as a strike against a man entering a religious order.) Devastated, he accepted a teaching position at St. Bonaventure's University, in Allegany, New York, a Franciscan school where he began to lead an almost monastic life while still a layman. Living in a small room at the college, he prayed more frequently, gave up smoking, and found that his soul gradually became "in harmony with itself."

Around this time, an instructor at Columbia suggested that Tom might make a retreat at a Trappist monastery near Bardstown, Kentucky, called the Abbey of Our Lady of Gethsemani. His visit to Gethsemani in the fall of 1941 stunned him. "This is the center of all the vitality in America," he wrote. "This is the cause and reason why the nation is holding together." In a few months, Tom entered the Trappists, to spend the rest of his life in this community, living under the vows of obedience, stability and *conversio morum*, or "conversion of manners," an assent to the monastic ways of poverty and chastity.

Merton, knowing himself to be a self-centered man, expected to be lost in the anonymity of the Kentucky monastery. Upon his entrance, he became Brother M. Louis Merton, OCSO (for "Order of the Cistercians of the Strict Observance," the formal name of the Trappist order). But his abbot (a term meaning "Father"), the head of the monastery, urged Merton to begin writing his memoirs. In 1948, his autobiography, *The Seven Storey Mountain*, was published. It became a bestseller almost immediately.

Thus Merton's life changed again, and he became, as he put it, ruefully, "the famous Thomas Merton."

The next few years of Merton's life are detailed in *The Sign of Jonas*, a compendium of journal entries that recounts his growing into his monastic vocation. In many ways, Merton's life in the monastery was no different than that of the other Trappists at Gethsemani. He completed his novitiate training and, in 1948, was ordained a deacon and, later that same year, a priest. In 1954 he was named "master" of the scholastics, or the young monks in training and, the following year, master of novices, an important position in the monastery. But with each new book he published, Merton's fame grew, and he began to receive a steady stream of letters and visitors.

A frequent theme in Merton's journals and letters around this time is the tensions inherent in his life at Gethsemani. He questioned his monastic vocation as much as he embraced it. He desired solitude as much as he craved attention and affection from his brothers. He sought intimacy with others as much as he treasured his chastity. He battled with his religious superiors as much as he hoped to follow his vow of obedience. Most of all, he wished for fame and influence as much as he saw that humility was the foundation for a healthy monastic life.

In all these things, Merton sought greater spiritual freedom. As the late M. Basil Pennington (himself a Trappist monk and abbot) puts it in his book *Thomas Merton: Brother Monk*: "His whole life was a quest for freedom — the freedom to be open to the wonderful reality that God has made, to God himself, to what is!"

In this way, Merton was on the road to becoming what he would call his "true self."

Thomas Merton would live the remaining twenty-seven years of his life as a Trappist at the Abbey of Our Lady of Gethsemani. During those years, he would write many books and essays on a great variety of topics: the contemplative life, early Christian theology, Zen Buddhism, nonviolence, poetry, the Cold War, and the life of the church. He maintained an exhaustive and exhausting correspondence with writers and thinkers from around the world and became a guiding light for many during the Cold War and the Vietnam War.

In 1965, Merton became a hermit on the grounds of the monastery. His little hermitage, at first a plain cinder-block building with a working fireplace but no bathroom, seems to have brought him greater peace — as well as some greater agitation as he struggled to live with himself. (The larger monastery

community had always moderated some of his natural impul-
siveness.) He had plenty of time to pray, could write when he
wanted, was able to spend time with the other monks, and could
receive a moderate number of visitors more easily.

An important part of this phase of his life, absent from
some early biographies, was Merton's falling in love in 1966 with
a nurse in a hospital during one of his many visits. (Merton suffered from poor health for much of his life.) After a turbulent
period, Merton recommitted himself to his monastic vows.

Toward the end of his life, Merton, the monk who
took a vow of stability, felt the desire to travel, but his abbot usually denied the requests. In 1968, he was given permission by a
new abbot to travel to the Far East. Since his college days, he had
been interested in Eastern religions and spirituality, and had
made a special study of Zen Buddhism while at Gethsemani.
Merton's trip took him to California, to Alaska, to India, and to
Ceylon, where, in front of a statue of the Buddha, he had a
deeply prayerful and mystical experience.

During an interfaith conference in Bangkok,
Thailand, Merton gave a brief lecture and then left the group.
He had lunch and then took a bath. A cry was heard from his
room and he was found in his bedroom, lying on the floor and
grasping an electric fan. Merton had come out of the bathtub,
slipped on the tiled floor, and grabbed a fan to break his fall. The
fan electrocuted him and he died instantly. He was fifty-three
years old. Merton's body was carried back to the monastery on a
U.S. military plane that, with a strange irony, also carried the
bodies of the dead soldiers from the Vietnam War.

Thomas Merton's grave at Gethsemani is a plain one, marked, like all the Trappist graves, with a simple white cross. His reads, "Fr. Louis Merton. Died December 10, 1968." He lies under the green grass, with his Trappist brothers, very near the abbey church.

Chapter Two

The Story of a (Corporate) Soul

Before going further, I should point something out. Despite any stereotypes anyone may have about the Jesuits, I am not an academic or a scholar. As Saint Paul would say, "By no means!" I do not have multiple doctorates, as do some of my Jesuit brothers. I don't even have *one*. I don't publish in any scholarly journals. I am not tenured anywhere, nor have I ever taught in a college or university or high school.

So I won't be able to propose any sophisticated theological hypotheses on Thomas Merton or the true self based on years of groundbreaking scholarly research. I'm not going to propose *anything* academic, as a matter of fact. Besides, there are plenty of good books written by scholars who have studied Merton's writings for years and years. It is fair to say that Merton has been written about more than he wrote—which is quite something, when you think about his prodigious output.

In any event, I'm no academic and so would never try to match the research of the great scholars who have written about Merton. All I have to offer is my own experience, my own reading of Thomas Merton, and what his writings on the true self have meant in my own spiritual life.

Yet Merton said many times that when it comes to spirituality, experience is *the* place to start. And my experience with Merton has taught me a great deal about what it means to be holy and what it means to be yourself. In short, Merton tells us a lot about what it means to become a saint. With that in mind, let's start with experience.

You could say that my own vocation to the Jesuits was born at Corpus Christi Church in New York City: specifically, at the baptismal font in the rear of the church, the spot where Thomas Merton was baptized in 1938. And though I have spent a good deal of my adult life in New York, it was only recently that I first came upon that icon of Merton's life.

After moving to New York as a Jesuit, whenever I was passing through the neighborhood, I would make a special trip to Corpus Christi, hoping to visit the place where Merton's life started anew. But, for some reason, the church was closed every time I visited. So during each visit I had to content myself with seeing the imposing red door of the church, which Merton wrote about in *The Seven Storey Mountain.*

As Merton explains in his book, he was sitting in his dormitory room reading about the Jesuit poet Gerard Manley Hopkins. Thinking about the poet's conversion to Catholicism, Merton suddenly was seized with the idea that he should finally be baptized. "I had nine blocks to walk," he writes. "Then I turned the corner of 121st Street, and the brick church and the presbytery was before me. I stood in the doorway and rang the bell and waited."

Seeing the inside of the church started to become something of an obsession, since I had already visited the other places where Merton had stayed while a young man living in New York City. I made numerous pilgrimages, for example, to the modest brick building on Perry Street in Greenwich Village where Merton rented rooms as a graduate student, and which looks exactly as it did in one of Merton's pen-and-ink drawings done in the 1930s. But just two years ago, the mother of a Jesuit in my community died, and the funeral was scheduled to be held at Corpus Christi.

Arriving there early on a bitterly cold January morning, I was greeted by the pastor. When I told him of my interest in Merton, he pointed to the rear of the church and said, "You know, that's where he was baptized."

Touching the rim of that cold marble font was a deeply moving moment for me, and an immensely satisfying one, too. For it was Thomas Merton's writings, specifically *The Seven Storey Mountain* and *No Man Is An Island* that led me to where I am today and helped me become the person I was meant to be.

I did not grow up in a very religious family. We were Catholics to be sure—Philadelphia Catholics, to be more specific—but we were not the kind of family given over to things like daily Mass, grace at meals, evening prayers, recitation of the Rosary, and the like. As a matter of fact, my father sometimes used to drive my sister and me to Sunday Masses at our parish church, drop us off, and stay in his car to read the Sunday paper. It seems funny now but back then it made perfect sense. "I've been to Mass enough for one lifetime," he once joked. "When you're an adult you can stop going to Mass, too." Now, lest you think I'm about to launch into a litany of childhood complaints, my parents were loving and kind, but they simply were not particularly religious.

Until my confirmation at age eleven, I dutifully attended CCD, a kind of Sunday School for Catholic children and adolescents attending public schools. But shortly afterward, I stopped going, since I had gotten what I wanted: first holy communion and confirmation.

Around that time, I also received my first rosary beads, which I hung on my bedpost and which I tried to pray when I couldn't fall asleep at night. Occasionally, I would forget to place it back on the bedpost in the morning, and it would fall out of the sheets and end up on the floor. My mother used to scold me for this, since she was the one who kept picking it up. One day she accidentally ran over my rosary beads with the vacuum cleaner. When she pulled it out, it had lost three beads. When I came home from school I spied it on my bedpost and said, "Hey look what happened to my rosary beads!" Hoping to make me feel better, she said, "Well, look on the bright side. Now it won't take you so long to pray it!"

Not long afterward, I noticed an advertisement in a magazine for a statue of Saint Jude, the patron saint of hopeless causes. I can't begin to imagine which magazine this might have been, since my parents weren't in the habit of leaving Catholic publications lying around the house, but, apparently, the photo of the statue was sufficiently appealing to convince me to drop $3.50 in an envelope. I also can't imagine what led me to focus my childish desires on Saint Jude and spend in excess of three weeks' allowance on a plastic statue instead of, say, another Archie comic book. My only other obsession at that time, as I recall, was a green pup tent I had seen in the Sears catalogue, but this too was thrown over in favor of Saint Jude.

In a few weeks, I received a little brown package in the mail. It contained a nine-inch-tall beige plastic statue, along with a booklet of prayers to be used while praying to the patron saint of hopeless causes. Saint Jude the Beige, who held a staff and carried a sort of plate with a face on it (which I supposed was Jesus but couldn't tell), was given pride of place on top of the dresser in my bedroom.

At that age, I was in the habit of praying to God only intermittently, and then mainly to ask for things. That is, "Let me get an 'A' on my next test." "Let me do well in Little League this year." "Let me be more popular." That kind of thing.

I used to imagine God as the Great Problem Solver, the one who would fix everything if I just prayed hard enough, used the right prayers, and prayed in precisely the right way. God was powerful, I thought, but also distant. And if the Great Problem Solver couldn't fix things, which seemed to occur more frequently than I would have liked, I turned to Saint Jude. I figured that if it was beyond the capacity of God to do something, then *surely* it must be a hopeless cause, and it was time to call on Saint Jude.

For most of my childhood, then, my religious life consisted in going to church very occasionally, praying the Rosary, and asking God and Saint Jude for help. Saint Jude stood patiently atop my dresser for ten years, until high school. My high school friends, when visiting our house, often used to hang out in my bedroom, and though I was by that point rather fond of Saint Jude, I was afraid of what my friends might say if they saw a strange plastic statue standing on my dresser. So Saint Jude was stuffed inside my sock drawer, and was brought out of the drawer only on special occasions.

My faith was another thing, you might say, that was also relegated to the sock drawer for the next several years. During high school, I went to Mass a few times a month, but even that moderate level of religiosity eventually tapered off. And as my faith grew thinner, my affinity for Saint Jude, the Rosary, the Eucharist, prayer, and the rest of it began to seem a little childish: silly, superstitious, and faintly embarrassing.

So, when I entered the Jesuits, at age twenty-seven, I did so with only an eleven-year-old's knowledge about the faith. This is where many American Catholics find themselves these days: confirmed, but not fully catechized. And when your novice director tells you to make sure there are enough purificators and corporals for the Mass, and you don't know what he's talking about, it's pretty embarrassing.

But I'm getting ahead of myself. When I entered college at the University of Pennsylvania, I started going to church more regularly—say, once or twice a month. And from time to time, I would pray to God, asking for this or that thing: a good grade, a good job, and so on. My relationship with God still revolved mainly around my asking for stuff.

I was still what you might call pretty unreligious. And unreflective as well. In college, I decided on a course of studies based on what everyone else was doing, and what I thought would get me the best job. So I enrolled in the Wharton School of Business at Penn, and majored in finance, and did fairly well. Unfortunately, there was no one around to ask, "Do you like what you're doing?" Or "What do you want to do for a career?"

Or, more basically, "Who do you want to *be*?"

Had someone asked me about discovering my true self, I would have surely laughed.

Still following the pack after graduation, I took a job at General Electric in New York City. The position was in international finance and accounting, and consisted mainly of toting up long lists of numbers, issuing reports that no one read, and making endless pages of accounting entries. It was dull work, and almost as soon as I started I longed to escape. By this point, my faith had became just a dimly burning flame, barely noticeable in my life. I still prayed to the Great Problem Solver, though, calling on God whenever I needed one thing or another: a big raise, a better apartment, a less crazy boss.

To hedge my bets, I attended Saint Vincent Ferrer Church, a parish run by the Dominican order that was near my apartment in Manhattan. As further testimony to how clueless I was, during the novitiate I met a Jesuit priest who remarked, after I told him about Saint Vincent's, "Well, you must have known the Dominicans there." I thought he meant people from the Dominican Republic, and I said, "Well, it was mostly white people when I was going there."

I stayed in New York for a few years with G.E. and eventually took a position with their office in Stamford, Connecticut. Finally, after six years of life in corporate America, I had to admit that I was miserable: overworked, stressed, lonely, and feeling trapped. My life had no discernible purpose or meaning. I remember thinking this: I go to work so I can make money so I can go to work. The logic of it was depressingly circular. Now, I have plenty of friends who still enjoy working in the business world, but that way of life simply wasn't for me, and I wanted out.

The only problem was that I couldn't see a way out.

One evening, I came home and flipped on the television set. The local PBS station was airing a documentary about a Catholic priest named Thomas Merton. Though I had never heard of Merton, a parade of talking heads appeared onscreen to testify to his influence on their lives. In just a few minutes, I got the idea that Merton was bright, funny, holy, and altogether unique. But there was something else about the show that drew me. It was the expression on his face: Thomas Merton's face seemed to radiate a peace that was wholly unknown to me. His face seemed to say: "See, I am happy." The documentary was sufficiently interesting to prompt me to track down, purchase, and read his autobiography, *The Seven Storey Mountain*. It captivated me as no book ever had.

Merton's autobiography leads the reader from the very beginning of his life, in France, through his sad and lonely boyhood, through his education at the *lycée* in France, at Oakham, at Cambridge, at Columbia, through his conversion, and through his ultimate entrance into the Trappists. It is very much the book of a young and zealous convert. Merton is certain that Catholicism is the only true faith, certain that he has made the right and the only decision, and certain that he is following God's will. Yet even in its excess of certainty, the book reached me as no other book ever had. Or ever has. Here was a man, roughly my own age, who had struggled with the same things I did: pride, disappointment, confusion, doubt, sadness, loneliness. More important, here was someone who seemed to have found an answer to discovering who he really was.

As I read his story, Merton's journey became, in a way, my journey. When I reached the point in the book where he walked through the door of Corpus Christi to begin the process of becoming Catholic, I found myself growing excited. When Merton was baptized, I thought, "Finally!" And a few pages later, when he reached to the door of the Abbey of Gethsemani, I again thought, "Finally!" But this time that "finally" seemed to apply to myself as well. In other words, I started to get the idea that what he had done was what I should do.

From then on, I read everything by Merton that I could get my hands on, as well as anything else that seemed even remotely relevant to living a spiritual life. I read *Surprised by Joy*, the memoir of the early life of C. S. Lewis; *The Diary of a Country Priest*, a novel by the French author Georges Bernanos; and *The Brothers Karamazov*, by Fyodor Dostoyevsky. I even read the Gospels!

This was of course the beginning of a vocation to religious life. To use the language of contemporary spirituality, God was at work through my deepest desires. It was also the beginning of the long journey to becoming my true self.

But I didn't see it that way. At the time, it all seemed to be, at best, a pipe dream, and at worst, insane. There was a big problem, too: I didn't seem to be made for a life like the one that Thomas Merton had led. That's not what my background or education had prepared me to become at all. So I was stuck. To paraphrase Merton in his book *The Sign of Jonas*, all of my training pointed one way, and all of my ideals the other.

Then, I found another of Merton's books, a series of meditations called *No Man Is an Island*. The book mystified me. It didn't seem to have any structure or any sort of theme. It was just Merton thinking aloud about things like despair, hope, and freedom. The chapters had mysterious titles like "The Word of the Cross" and "The Wind Blows Where It Pleases." What did that mean?

Flipping through the book late one night, after another miserable day at work, I stumbled upon the following passage in a chapter entitled "Being and Doing":

> Why do we have to spend our lives striving to be something we would never want to be, if we only knew what we wanted? Why do we waste our time doing things which, if we only stopped to think about them, are just the opposite of what we were made for?

And I thought, "Hey, that's *me!*"

That passage, which I return to frequently, marked a turning point. It was a real "Aha!" moment. Merton had given my feelings a language: I wasn't made for the life I was in. There I was, "striving to be something I would never want to be."

Those few lines led me to seriously consider changing everything in my life, they led me to a greater interest in spirituality, and they eventually led me to consider the priesthood and then a religious order, and, finally, they led me to enter the Society of Jesus, more commonly known as the Jesuits.

It was a long process, not without its doubts and confusions and frustrations and dead ends, but in the end, it seemed to me that the Jesuit way of life would be a good deal more satisfying than the corporate way of life. And I figured, well, I might as well try it out. So six years after graduating from college and two years after encountering Thomas Merton, I entered the Jesuit novitiate. It was certainly the best decision I've ever made, and, amazingly, it seemed that God had made the decision for me. I hadn't sought an answer to the problem at all. The Great Problem Solver, as it turned out, had been at work on a problem that I had only dimly comprehended.

Chapter Three

True Selves and False Ones

T homas Merton continued to be a big help after I entered the novitiate. His simple concept of the true self, the person we are before God and the person we are meant to be, was a critical insight in my spiritual life. Those lines about "striving to be something that we would never want to be" continued to be part of my daily meditation.

Overall, the quest both to understand oneself and finally accept oneself was a key journey for me as a Jesuit novice. Interestingly, the very next line after that passage I mentioned from *No Man is an Island* is this: "We cannot become ourselves unless we know ourselves." So I set out on the quest to know myself. In fact, I had begun that journey in earnest on the day that I first started reading *The Seven Storey Mountain*, but, back then, I didn't see it that way. If you had asked me, I would have probably said that I was simply trying to "escape" from my old life.

It is probably more accurate to describe what was going on as a gradual movement toward becoming the true self and away from the false self. Before coming to know the true self, one must confront the false self that one has usually spent a lifetime constructing and nourishing.

In his book *New Seeds of Contemplation,* Merton wrote, "Every one of us is shadowed by an illusory person: the false self." With his typical insight, Merton identifies the false self as the person that we wish to present to the world, and the person we want the whole world to revolve around:

> Thus I use up my life in the desire for pleasures and the thirst for experiences, for power, honor, knowledge and love, to clothe this false self and construct its nothingness into something objectively real. And I wind experiences around myself and cover myself with pleasures and glory like bandages in order to make myself perceptible to myself and to the world, as if I were an invisible body that could only become visible when something visible covered its surface.

This notion of being "clothed" with the bandages of the false self, like the Invisible Man being wrapped, mummy-like, in long, winding strips of cloths, struck a deep chord within me. The self that I had long presented to others — the person interested in climbing the corporate ladder, in always being clever and hip, in knowing how to order the best wines, in attending the hottest parties, and in getting into the hippest clubs, in never doubting my place in the world, in always being, in a word, *cool* — that person was unreal. That person was nothing more than a mask I wore. And I knew it.

I had known it for some time, too.

One warm day in spring, during senior year in college, I was walking jauntily across campus to a job interview dressed in a new suit and tie. On one level, I felt confident. Assured. Certain. Just about to finish up my degree at Wharton, I had a full slate of job interviews lined up with some of the world's biggest companies. In a few months I would be making lots of money, possibly have my own office, and be set for life. Over my arm I was carrying an expensive new khaki raincoat that I had just bought for interviewing season.

On my way, I passed a good friend. She took one look at me and said, "Wow, you look like you're carrying a prop." I felt unmasked.

Of course, almost any college student would probably feel strange in that situation; everyone I knew felt as if they were doing a bit of playacting when it came to interviews. But my friend's words struck at a deeper level: I felt as if those bandages that I had wrapped around me had suddenly been stripped away. My heart knew that as much as I *wanted* to want this, I wasn't made for the life that I was supposed to want.

Now, I should note that business is a fine vocation for a great many people—many of my friends, in fact. The point is not that business is somehow bad, but rather that this life was pretty much the opposite of what I wanted to be doing. Yet I had created, over many years, this persona, this other self, which I thought would be pleasing to everyone: to my family, my friends, my professors. And this "false self," separated from my true desires, was sure that a life in corporate America was the right path. This false self was sure about everything.

I love what Richard Rohr, the Franciscan priest, says about this in his book *Adam's Return:* "Our false self is who we *think* we are. It is our mental self-image and social agreement, which most people spend their whole lives living up to—or down to."

Keeping this false self alive requires a good deal of work. And for me, it was an almost all-consuming effort. It took work to convince people that I was all the things I wanted them to think I was: "Of course I can't wait to start my job!" It took work to make sure that no one saw me as uncertain about any-thing in life, especially in my professional life. "Of course I love reading *The Wall Street Journal!*" It took work to run away from my true desires, my true feelings, and my true vocation in life: "Of course I love my job!"

The "clothing" of yourself with these bandages, in Merton's phrase, also means that if you are not ever vigilant, those bandages may occasionally slip, and reveal your underly-ing true self to others. A few years after beginning my work at General Electric, I used to doodle on my desk this note, over and over, in small letters: "I hate my life." How sad it is to remember that. But it felt that this was the only way I could express myself.

One friend, sitting at my desk one evening, noticed these scribblings. It was around 10 at night, and we were horsing around, laughing and throwing wadded-up pieces of paper at each other. Letting off steam after a tiring day. He glanced down at my desk. In an instant, his face dropped and a wave of pity crossed his face. "Do you really hate your life?" he said quietly.

How strange it felt to sit across from my friend. How strange it felt for my false self to be revealed, to have the band-ages slip and show my real feelings. I longed to be honest with him. There were two choices: to be honest and share myself with another person, or to lie and conceal myself from my friend. I chose the second option. "What?" I said.

He pointed to the words I had written. Looking over his shoulder, I pretended to read them for the first time. "Oh," I said, carefully rearranging the bandages of my false self, "I was just having a bad day, you know?" The false self had reasserted itself. Those bandages would not fall away for many years.

The trajectory of Merton's own life clearly shows his own steady movement away from the false self. This is perhaps most evident in his gradual acceptance and understanding of his vocation as a Trappist monk.

Merton's early journals and letters are filled with a confidence that unsuccessfully masks a deep longing for a place to belong. These feelings continue unabated until the day he enters the monastery, when he finally finds the home he has long been searching for. But even then, during his years at the abbey, even after he has become a monk, Merton continues to meditate on what *kind* of monk he is intended to be, as he moves closer toward being the person God intended him to be. His spiritual journey was far from complete when he entered the doors of the abbey. In many ways it had just begun.

But it was not a solitary journey. Indeed, Merton speaks of this journey as "discovering myself in discovering God." Ultimately, he says, "If I find Him I will find myself, and if I find my true self I will find Him." In other words, God desires for us to be the persons we were created to be: to be simply and purely ourselves, and in this state to love God and to let ourselves be loved by God. It is a double journey, really: finding God means allowing ourselves to be found by God. And finding our true selves means allowing God to find and reveal our true selves to us.

Those spiritual phrases may sound overly abstract and overly pious, and maybe even a little hollow and hokey. What does this mean on a practical level? And how does one put that insight into action?

Simply put, one attempts to move *away* from those parts of ourselves that prevent us from being closer to God: self-

ishness, pride, fear, and so on. And one also tries, as far as possible, to move *toward* those parts of ourselves that draw us nearer
to God. In the process, one gradually finds oneself growing more
loving and more generous. One also trusts that the very *desire* to
do this comes from God. That is, the desire for our true selves to
be revealed, and for us to move nearer to God, is a desire planted
within us by God.

At the same time, one's own individuality, one's own
brand of holiness is gradually revealed. Our personalities are not
eradicated as much as they are made fuller, more real, and finally
more holy. In his collection of essays entitled *Karl Rahner:
Spiritual Writings*, the esteemed Catholic theologian wrote,
"Christianity's sense of the human relationship to God is *not* one
that says that the more a person grows closer to God, the more
that person's existence vanishes into a puff of smoke."

In the quest for the true self, one therefore begins to
appreciate and accept one's personality and one's life as an essential way that God calls us to be ourselves. Everyone is called to sanctity in different ways—in often *very* different ways. The path to
sanctity for a young mother is different from that of an elderly
priest. Moreover, the path to sanctity for an extroverted young man
who loves nothing more than spending time with his friends cheer-
ing on their favorite baseball team over a few beers is probably very
different from that of the introspective middle-aged woman who
likes nothing better than to sit at home on her favorite chair with a
good book and a pot of chamomile tea. One's personal brand of
holiness becomes clearer the more the true self is revealed.

And as we move closer to becoming our true selves,
the selves we are meant to be, the selves that God created, the
more loving parts of us are naturally magnified, and the more
sinful parts are naturally diminished. As are so many other blocks

to true freedom. As Richard Rohr writes, "Once you learn to live as your true self, you can never be satisfied with this charade again: it then feels so silly and superficial."

By the way, this may anticipate an important critique of the notion of the true self. Just recently, when I told another Jesuit about this book, he asked, "Well, that's fine, but what happens if your true self is a horrible, lying, mean-spirited person?"

My answer was that this would not be the person God created. In other words, to find his true self, the horrible, lying, mean-spirited person would have to uncover his true self—the good self that God created—from underneath all those layers of sinfulness. And I would suspect that the longer he had been living as a selfish person, the longer it might take for him to uncover his true self.

Over the course of his life, Merton, for example, became a more expansive and generous person, and, likewise, his intolerance of others diminished over time. This was an outgrowth of his quest to be himself and to move closer to God. And it is evident in his writings.

In *The Secular Journal,* for example, the collection of journals from the 1930s and 1940s that immediately preceded Thomas Merton's entrance into the Trappists, the reader meets a clever young man full of enthusiasm and strongly held beliefs on literature, art, politics, people, and, in time, religion. The reader also meets a young man who is sometimes insufferably smug. (It is a testimony to Merton's humility that he allowed some of the smuggest passages to remain in his manuscript.)

There is, for example, a cringe-inducing entry detailing his visit to the New York World's Fair in 1939. In his journal, he recounts his reactions as he observes the crowds observing some notable paintings that have been sent over for exhibition at the Fair. It is a merciless portrait of Merton's fellow human beings, who are depicted as far less sophisticated than the writer. He even mocks some of them for not being able to correctly pronounce the name of the Flemish artist Peter Bruegel, who painted in the sixteenth century.

> There were a lot of people who just read the name: "Broo-gul," and walked on unabashed. . . . They came across with the usual reaction of people who don't know pictures are there to be enjoyed, but think they are things that have to be learned by heart to impress the bourgeoisie: so they tried to remember the name.

The possibility that among those crowds were people who appreciated what they were seeing is entirely lost on the young Merton. The idea that he might give them the benefit of the doubt is likewise absent.

A few years later, in *The Seven Storey Mountain*, Merton reveals more of his youthful and occasionally patronizing attitudes, particularly when it comes to other religions. Though one could find some "sincere charity" among Quakers, the Society of Friends is summed up in a few dismissive lines: "But when I read the works of William Penn and found them to be as supernatural as the Montgomery Ward catalog, I lost interest in the Quakers." Ironically, Eastern spirituality, which would play a great role in Merton's later life, is similarly dismissed. After a discussion about his attempts at self-hypnosis, he writes, "Ultimately, I suppose all Oriental mysticism can be reduced to techniques that do the same thing, but in a far more subtle and advanced fashion: and if that is true it is not mysticism at all." So much for *that* spiritual tradition! But Merton grants them this: "That does not make it evil *per se...*" How generous of him!

Still, unlike his earlier writings, buried within *The Seven Storey Mountain* is Merton's awareness that his arrogance is not motivated by love. He begins to realize how much his responses to people stem from his own shortcomings. After he criticizes the services at the Zion Church near his grandparents' house in Douglaston, Long Island, he recognizes that his own pride "increased the irritation and complicated it."

How different all of this is from the later Merton! After several years in the monastery, he began to soften to other people, to other viewpoints, and even to "the world," which had previously stood for all that was bad in life. Merton's true self, the loving person buried under his arrogance and his hurt, began to be revealed, so that even people that he did not know were seen in the light of their relationship to God. The more time he spent with God, the more generous he became. His true self was a generous self.

Compare his experience with those museumgoers in 1939 with his famous epiphany in Louisville in 1958. He writes about this in his book *Conjectures of a Guilty Bystander*. Merton has just been into town to see a doctor. Standing on a busy intersection he finds this:

> In Louisville, at the corner of Fourth and Walnut, in the center of the shopping district, I was suddenly overwhelmed with the realization that I loved all those people, that they were mine and I theirs, that we could not be alien to one another even though we were total strangers. It was like awaking from a dream of separateness, of spurious self-isolation in a special world, the world of renunciation and supposed holiness.

It is no wonder that in later life Thomas Merton said that he no longer knew the man who wrote *The Seven Storey Mountain.* The person who years before had stood apart from the crowds is now firmly in their midst, loving them. The true self can now contemplate the false self with some distance, some wisdom, and even some compassion.

Chapter Four

So Who Am I, Anyway?

Entering the Jesuits was, for me, a step toward removing the bandages that had clothed the false self. It was also a step toward revealing the identity of the true self.

Those lines may sound pretty arrogant, for at least two reasons. First, it is always God who invites us to that kind of freedom. What was going on in the Jesuit novitiate was a continuation of the original call that God was holding out for me. As with any spiritual journey, I was not the instigator of the trip. Second, the statement that I *began* to move toward the true self should not be taken to mean that I have already *reached* that point! To quote Saint Paul again, "By no means!" I am still full of many things that keep me from being who I am meant to be. In the language of spiritual writers, I am still full of "unfreedoms," "disordered attachments," "tendencies to sinfulness," and just plain old "sin." So I am very much still traveling along that road, finding my way, like everyone else. But I would be dishonest if I said that entering the Jesuit novitiate did not prompt me to do some serious thinking about who I was meant to be.

So who was I supposed to be, anyway? What was my true self? And how was I supposed to discover him, or it, or whatever it was? Merton wrote that the quest for the true self is part of the quest to let God know you as you are. But when I first read those lines I wasn't sure what they meant or how to go about putting them into action. Fortunately, I had some good spiritual directors to help me along the way.

Much of this journey involved my letting go of the need to be somebody else. Nobody in particular, mind you, just a feeling that I needed to be *different.* Early in the novitiate, I thought that being holy meant changing an essential part of who I was, *suppressing* my personality, not building on it. I was eradicating my natural desires and inclinations, rather than asking God to sanctify and even perfect them. Here's the way I thought about it: I knew that I certainly wasn't a holy person, so therefore being holy must mean being a different person.

As strange as it sounds, I thought that being myself meant being someone else.

For example, I would notice that another novice whom I admired was quiet and soft-spoken and diffident and introspective. I would think, "I need to be quiet and soft-spoken and diffident and introspective." Consequently, the following days were spent in a largely useless attempt at being quiet, until someone would eventually say, "Are you feeling all right?" The very next week I would meet someone who had a particular fondness for praying very early in the morning, and who seemed very holy, and I would say to myself, "Well, I guess I have to start praying early in the morning, too." And then, up at five in the morning for my new regime, until that tired me out, too.

My spiritual director kept reminding me that I didn't really need to be like anyone else except me. But it took a while for that to sink in.

Beside a lingering sense that I wasn't worthy of being a Jesuit, there was a good deal of envy in my attitude. At various times in my life, especially when things were not going so well, I have been envious and even jealous of other people. At heart, my envy boiled down to this: everyone else has it easier than I do. And so they are so obviously happier than I am!

Of course this is false, and dangerous, too. One tends to compare one's own life, which is always a mixed bag of good and bad, with what one falsely perceives as the "perfect life" of the other. In this way, we minimize our own gifts and graces and maximize the other person's. Ironically, we often do the opposite with our problems and struggles: we maximize our own and minimize the other person's. Others seem more clever, more attractive, more popular, more relaxed, more athletic, more whatever, than we are and therefore (or so it seems) they lead a charmed life. Likewise, the other person, we surmise, faces no real problems in his or her life. Or if we know that they do face problems, we think, "Well, their problems are not as bad as mine."

But no one leads that proverbial "charmed life." Everyone's life is a full measure of graces and blessings, as well as struggles and challenges. And if we consistently compare our own complicated reality with the supposed perfection of another's life, is it any wonder that we wish we were other than who we are? A brief conversation with anyone about their problems will convince you of this reality.

Longer conversations are even better. When people began coming to me for spiritual counseling, I was astonished not simply at the ways that God blesses others, but at how difficult everyone's life is. How much everyone has to struggle to be loved, to be accepted, and to be happy. Not long ago a man who I greatly admired came to see me. He seemed to have everything:

a good job, a loving wife, two wonderful children. But after speaking with him for just a few minutes, it became very clear that his life was far from easy. In fact, as he poured out his heart, I saw his life as actually more difficult than my own, something that I would never have predicted.

Around the same time, I began spending time with an acting company in New York City that was putting together an off-Broadway play called *The Last Days of Judas Iscariot*, by Stephen Adly Guirgis, which examined the relationship between Jesus and Judas. Here was a group of talented and successful people—actors, directors, playwrights—who many would say led a "charmed" life. And their lives were in many ways rich and full ones. At the same time, they struggled with the same things that everyone does, faced difficult challenges, endured sadnesses and frustrations, and certainly didn't see their own lives as either charmed or easy or perfect. They worked hard (harder than I could have imagined—one actress spent her mornings and after-noons filming a television show and her evenings on stage). And they had to face the same essential spiritual poverty that all of us face: the poverty of knowing our own human limitations.

It was another example of how wrong it is to idealize another person's situation. (At one point, one of the actors said to me, "You're lucky you lead the life you do!") In other words, no one's life is free of suffering.

The tendency to compare is a great trap in the spiritual life, especially today, when much in our culture tempts us to think that if only we were someone else—better looking, better educated, better moneyed—we would be happier. All we need to do is to be other than who we are.

Why is this such a dangerous temptation? For many reasons. First, because it leads to despair. Trapped by our false ways of perceiving other people's lives, we denigrate our own lives, and thus devalue ourselves. And since it is always easier to imagine the "fantasy" life of the other, we remain stubbornly unsatisfied with our own. The tendency to compare ultimately leads to despair, since our own real life can never compare with the perceived (but false) perfection of the other person's life. And so we are led into a spiritual dead end. There is a pithy saying for this: "Compare and despair."

The tendency to make false comparisons is unhealthy because it also leads us away from the true self, and encourages us to be someone else, someone whom God did not create. This is not to say that one cannot admire good and holy people and desire to emulate them in some way. One might read the lives of the saints and think: I could be more generous, more loving, more patient, and so on. But, when we think that we have to *become* them in order to be holy, we are denying the person whom God has created.

One is freed from this spiritual prison not only by reflecting more realistically on the sometimes painful lot of others, as well as accompanying them into their suffering, but also by reflecting on the blessings in our own lives. In other words, by engaging in the practice of gratitude.

In the novitiate, this meant reminding myself that the way God had made me wasn't so bad after all. While I wasn't the silent and diffident type I admired, I had a certain degree of extroversion and humor that others in the community told me they enjoyed. And while I didn't rise at five in the morning to begin my prayers, I was able to see my own life of prayer as rich in its own way. (As an added benefit, I was able to sleep later, too!) The gifts and talents and natural desires that had been placed in me by God were valued by others and needed to be valued by me.

My journey was also inadvertently encouraged by other novices. The novice I admired for his quiet demeanor said to me at the end of the year, "I wish I were as outgoing as you are!"

For many, the road to self-acceptance can be arduous. For instance, those of ethnic minorities, with physical disabilities, or with painful family backgrounds may find the temptation to compare overwhelming. Still, the journey is an essential one in the spiritual life. Many gay men and lesbians, for example, have told me that a foundational part of their own spiritual development has been accepting themselves as gay men and women; that is, this is the way that God has made them. Coming to accept themselves in this way, and, more importantly, allowing God to love them *as they are*, not as they might wish they could be, or how society might want them to be, is an important step in one's relationship with God.

God loves us as we are because we are as God made us. "For I am fearfully and wonderfully made," says Psalm 139. I think that this is something of what the psalmist may have meant.

The notion of the true self also helped me in some practical ways, particularly when it came to ministry.

An important part of the Jesuit novitiate, for example, included working fifteen hours a week in a "ministerial" setting. Much of this work was to be with the poor in the area, and would help us understand the needs of the poor, as well as the graces that come from working with and alongside them. We called these ministries our "apostolates" (the kind of work that an apostle would do). When I used that word with my sister, she said, "Pasta-lites? Is that some sort of Italian restaurant or something?"

During my first fall as a novice, while I was still struggling with the idea of the true self, I was assigned to work at a large hospital in Cambridge, Massachusetts, about an hour's subway ride away from the novitiate. The hospital, run by the Grey Nuns, cared for seriously ill patients, many of whom suffered from multiple sclerosis, cancer, AIDS, the effects of serious head injuries, and so on.

I was terrified of working there. As someone who hated even *visiting* someone in the hospital, I could scarcely imagine myself working there. Ironically, this very fear sealed the novice director's decision to send me. There is an old Jesuit practice called *agere contra*, which means, in essence, "to act against." If there is a part of ourselves that is not free, we try to "act against" that part in order to free ourselves from resistance in that area. For example, if a novice fears working with homeless men and women, he may be asked to do just that, so as to invite him into the experience of finding God in that unexpected place and move past his fear. All of this is a way to grow in freedom and love. So when the novice director heard that I instinctively hated hospitals, he asked if my fear and revulsion might be something that I needed to be free of.

As an aside, this example points out the need for attentiveness and discernment in the quest to become our true selves. In this case, one could argue that, since I didn't want to work in a hospital, this was simply how God had made me and I should just accept it. (That is, you could argue that my true self just wasn't interested in hospital work.) But my novice director wisely saw that this resistance was really an unfreedom, something that would keep me from growing more as a loving person.

So how do you determine if something is an essential part of your true self or simply an unfreedom that needs to be challenged? Good question. Basically, one has to ask, "Is this part of myself keeping me from being more loving and generous? Is this keeping me from being closer to God and to other people?" If the answer is yes, perhaps it may be time to consider how you could move away from whatever prevents you from being more loving and generous.

Still, as I said, I was terrified.

Fortunately, I was to work alongside a well-trained pastoral care team who had been ministering to the patients there for many years, and had plenty of experience shepherding nervous Jesuit novices around.

At first, I barely knew what to say to the patients, all of whom suffered intensely. One woman, named Rita, had been living in the hospital for twenty years. Remember, said one pastoral care worker, going into her hospital room is like entering her house. Another young man, named Gene, had suffered severe head injuries from a motorcycle accident years before, and could communicate only with great difficulty by using a tray affixed to the arms of his wheelchair. When Gene wanted to say something, he would point to small letters pasted on the tray and laboriously spell out his sentences.

I had no idea what to do or say in these situations. In a few days, I could feel myself becoming tongue-tied with apprehension and almost paralyzed with doubt. What was the right thing to say? What if I said the wrong thing? What if something I said made them sad or, worse, angry with me? I started to dread the days that I was scheduled to work at the hospital.

Early on, I tried to imagine what an "experienced hospital chaplain" would do. So I would engage the patients in the types of "serious" conversations I would imagine would be helpful to them. For example, I thought an experienced chaplain would get Rita to discuss her condition with me. I would ask her about her physical ailments, about how she was feeling, and about how she was feeling about how she was feeling, and so on. Despite my persistent questions, though, it seemed that all Rita wanted to talk about was her brother, who was a Jesuit priest. But I thought that an experienced hospital chaplain wouldn't engage in such idle small talk. So I kept trying to steer her back to answering my serious questions.

One day I confessed this to Ernie, one of the pastoral care workers. He thought for a moment. "It's good that you want Rita to open up to you, and maybe she will one day. But why not just try being yourself?"

It was terrific advice. I stopped worrying about being the "experienced hospital chaplain" and started thinking that maybe God had placed me there for a reason: once again, not my idea of who I should be, but *me*.

So the next time Rita started talking about her brother, the priest, I joined right in, and asked what I would ask anyone: What's your brother like? Where does he work? How long has he been a Jesuit? What was it like for you when he entered the novitiate? We had a relaxed talk, even though she never mentioned her condition, or how she felt, or anything like that. But at the end of our conversation Rita said, "Can you come back tomorrow?"

Over the next few weeks, Rita began to share more of her life with me and, eventually, she did tell me about her condition and how she felt. Our relationship deepened after that.

That experience helped me to see that while Rita probably could have used an "experienced hospital chaplain," it was I who was there with her. God had put me beside her bed, and it was I whom God wanted there, for some reason. So, it was better to be myself. That doesn't mean that one shouldn't be properly prepared for a job—especially one as demanding as a hospital chaplain—but it does mean that one shouldn't lose sight of the importance of being one's true self in front of every person one meets.

Let me tell you a story that looks at this reality from a different perspective. I think it may show how even the parts of us that we think are worthless are what God sometimes puts to the best use.

When I entered the novitiate, I figured that I would never again use any of my business training. Many of my friends sang the same lament: all that studying at Wharton and six years of work in the corporate world down the drain! And while I was happy to have entered the Jesuits, I wondered if the last ten years of my life had been largely useless. That part of myself—the business part—that for so long had seemed desirable now seemed undesirable. It seemed a great waste of years of study and work. I began to feel foolish, as if I had made a colossal mistake in life, and wondered why I hadn't entered the Jesuits earlier.

A few years after the novitiate, though, I was sent to work with the Jesuit Refugee Service in Nairobi, Kenya. The Jesuits there were helping refugees who had migrated into Kenya from all over East Africa—from Rwanda, Sudan, Ethiopia, Uganda, and Somalia—fleeing famine and war. All of them lived in city's sprawling slums, and all of them were very poor.

When I arrived, however, it wasn't clear what my job would be. The Jesuit Refugee Service ran a number of programs for refugees living in Nairobi. There was the "parish-outreach program," which helped the city's parishes care for the huge numbers of refugees who had settled within their boundaries. They also managed a "medical-assistance program" that enabled refugees to get the medical care they needed for themselves and their families. And there was an extensive scholarship program that provided refugee families money to cover the exorbitant "school fees" that Kenya's public schools demanded at the time. (By the way, these programs were offered to all the refugees, not simply the Catholic ones.)

As it turned out, I was assigned to work with the scholarship program, run by an energetic German nun named Sister Luise. But on my very first day, Sister Luise admitted that she already employed four Sudanese refugees to help manage the scholarship program. She had an accountant, two caseworkers, and even a driver.

"So you see," she said, shrugging her shoulders, "I'm not sure what you could do here."

Though I didn't tell her so, I was furious. Had I come thousands of miles to be told that there was nothing for me to do? But after some long talks with my spiritual director, I decided to wait and see what God would present to me.

Over the next few months, I found myself getting more involved with another program that the Jesuits ran, called the "income-generating activities." This program offered small financial grants to groups of refugees to enable them to start their own small businesses, as a way of helping them support their families. When I arrived in Nairobi, there were perhaps a dozen of these little businesses. One group of Ugandan women had organized a small sewing cooperative that turned out brightly colored batiked shirts and dresses. A group of Rwandan women ran a little bread bakery in one of the city's more notorious slums. Two Ethiopian brothers ran a small restaurant, consisting of just a few wooden tables and makeshift stools.

The income-generating program was managed by an Austrian lay woman named Uta, who had previously worked with the Jesuit Refugee Service in a similar program in Southeast Asia. Since Sister Luise had little for me to do, I began spending more time with Uta, who welcomed any help with the ever-growing number of small businesses in Nairobi.

I enjoyed the work immensely. Uta and I would travel around the slums visiting each of the groups, checking up on them, offering them advice, encouraging them when things weren't going well, and celebrating with them when they were. The sheer variety of the projects enthralled me: besides the sewing projects, we sponsored refugees who worked together as basket-makers, carpenters, quilt-makers, woodcarvers, and book-binders. We even sponsored a tiny chicken farm housed in a little wooden shack. (Whenever we visited, we were immediately asked for advice on how to cure various chicken illnesses.)

In a few months, Uta and I began scouting around Nairobi for a house that could double as an office and a show-room for the various refugee handicrafts. We quickly found one on the grounds of a Jesuit-run parish on the outskirts of a large slum. A year after I arrived, we opened the "Mikono Centre" (after the Swahili word for *hands*). Between the many Catholic priests, brothers, and sisters who worked in the area, American and European expatriates, the international diplomatic corps, and wealthy Kenyans we knew, the shop did a marvelous business, and the refugees were delighted to find paying customers for their handicrafts.

To my amazement, I found myself constantly drawing on my business experience. Of course the new Mikono Centre needed to have its books and accounts set up, and we needed to do some marketing throughout the city. But we also needed to help teach the refugees themselves something about accounting, marketing, management, and the need for things like investing, keeping bank accounts, determining the correct price of merchandise, dealing with suppliers, and so on.

Every few months, I would run a "Business Seminar" for the refugees that reviewed the basics of how to run a small business. One important lesson, for example, was charging prices for their products that would at least cover the cost of what they had paid for supplies, plus whatever they needed to pay in salaries. After one seminar, the Rwandan bakers raised the price of the bread that they had been supplying to the local Jesuit community and the Mikono Centre staff.

The price of a loaf of bread jumped from four shillings to five shillings. When I asked why the price had been raised, the head of the cooperative said, "We listened to what you told us!"

The talents that I thought I had permanently left behind — my business skills — turned out to be of enormous help in my work in Nairobi. Moreover, they turned out to be enormously helpful to the refugees. In fact, I ended up using a wider variety of my business skills in Nairobi than I ever had in my job with General Electric.

Once again I realized that God can use *every* part of our selves — even those parts we think are useless — for the good. God writes straight, as the proverb goes, with crooked lines.

In each of these situations, I realized that I wasn't called to be the person I thought should have been sent there, or the person I thought would do a better job, I was just called to be myself, my *true self*. Throughout my Jesuit life, whether I was working in a hospital or a homeless shelter or a prison or a refugee camp, I discovered that I didn't have to ask myself, "What would Mother Teresa do?" or "What would Francis of Assisi do?" Certainly their lives are superb models for Christian action, but a better question is "What should *I* do?"

I tried to bring all of myself to each of these jobs: all my talents and skills and gifts, as well as my struggles and limitations and failings. I brought all of those things because that's who God brought there.

Overall, Thomas Merton's idea of the true self, the person who you are before God, gradually enabled me to see how God calls each of us in every situation to be ourselves: nothing more and, more importantly, nothing less.

Chapter Five

Writing the True Self

T he writings of Thomas Merton were of great help to me as a Jesuit novice. But there was another person who also helped me during that time in my life, someone I met shortly after I entered the novitiate: Henri Nouwen.

Many of Henri Nouwen's books lined the creaky wooden shelves of our novitiate library. One rainy Saturday afternoon, after our weekly housecleaning assignments had been completed, I chanced to pull down a book called *The Genesee Diary: Report from a Trappist Monastery*, by Henri Nouwen. Never having heard of Nouwen, I decided to read the book primarily because I liked the picture of the monastery on the cover. From this simple attraction, however, came an introduction to a person who helped me understand the true self almost as much as Merton had.

Since we're thinking about how individuals become themselves during their lives, it's probably a good idea to offer a very brief biography of Henri Nouwen, one of the towering figures of contemporary spirituality. Before his death in 1996, Nouwen authored over forty books on the spiritual life, which have already been translated into twenty-two languages.

Like Thomas Merton (whom he once met at the Abbey of Gethsemani), Henri Nouwen was a supremely talented man, a compassionate priest, a gifted writer, and certainly a spiritual master. But, also like Merton, Nouwen was a restless person, always seeking to find his place in the world. A friend once told me, bluntly, "I loved Henri, but he was probably the neediest human being I've ever met." In many ways, Nouwen's story is the story of a good man who struggled all his life to find his true self.

Nouwen was born in Holland in 1932 and, as early as age six, felt a desire to become a priest; his grandmother once made him a set of vestments and crafted a tiny altar so he could "celebrate" a Mass. Though he was educated at a Jesuit school, Henri decided not to become a Jesuit, because he thought it would require too much study. Instead he entered the diocesan seminary and was ordained for the diocese of Utrecht in 1957.

His early ordination, at age twenty-five, may have seemed the answer to all his vocation questions, holding out the promise of a life of stability and clarity. That goal, however, would prove elusive for Nouwen. Finding his true self would be an arduous lifelong journey, but would also become the basis for some of his most powerful writing.

Because of his interest in pastoral ministry, Nouwen was given permission by his bishop to study psychology immediately after his ordination. He enrolled at the University of Nijmegen, where he spent six years. Despite his best efforts, however, he did not complete his doctorate degree, and instead, in 1964, received a *doctorandus* degree, a kind of professional certification in psychology. Afterward, Nouwen worked for two years at the prestigious Menninger Clinic in Topeka, Kansas, in the Religion and Psychiatry Program. There he worked in clinical pastoral education, research, and writing. Around that time, Nouwen became more interested in the larger political world, joining Martin Luther King, Jr., in the great civil rights march from Selma to Montgomery, Alabama.

In 1966, Henri was invited to teach at the University of Notre Dame, where he spent two years helping to develop the new psychology department, as well as initiating courses in pastoral theology. It was at Notre Dame that his writing career began in earnest. Afterward he returned to the Netherlands, again to Nijmegen, to study theology. Balking at the requirement to write an academic thesis, he again received another *doctorandus*, a disappointment for him. But the personal setback did nothing to slow his professional ascent. For the next ten years, from 1971 through 1981, he taught at the Yale Divinity School, where he became one of the school's most popular professors.

Teaching at an avowedly Protestant seminary meant that Nouwen had the opportunity to adopt an ecumenical attitude, something that would eventually allow him to reach out to a much broader audience than just Catholics. As Michael O'Laughlin writes in his biography *God's Beloved: A Spiritual Biography of Henri Nouwen:* "[B]ecause Yale was a Protestant school, Henri was not only able but virtually compelled to take Catholic ecumenical advances onward to new levels, since most of the people to whom he was asked to minister were non-Catholic."

During his time at Yale, Nouwen wrote some of his most popular books, including *The Wounded Healer*, which, like much of his writing, was notable not only for its rich insights into the spiritual life, but also for its candor about the author's personal struggles. He also deepened his commitment to contemplative prayer and, in 1974, he wrote *The Genesee Diary*, an account of his seven months with the Trappist monks of the Abbey of Our Lady of the Genesee, in Piffard, New York. While at Genesee, Nouwen began to consider whether God might be asking him to give up some of his busy and increasingly stressful life of teaching, writing, and counseling. He found himself pulled in two separate directions: the exciting but hectic life of the public academic, and the peaceful but (to him) lonely life of the monk. After his time with the Trappists he decided to return to his position at Yale.

In the following years, Nouwen became increasingly interested in the political situation in Latin America. In 1981, he left Yale to spend six months in Peru, discerning whether to spend the rest of his life in South America, and also whether to join the Maryknoll Fathers, one of the largest Catholic missionary orders. It is easy to see that this time was one of intense struggle about his vocation, a further effort to understand his place in the world. Ultimately, Nouwen decided to return to his academic career. Still, this period led him to a deeper understanding of the place of social justice in the spiritual life. Out of this period came a journal that was published as *¡Gracias!*

Beginning in 1983, he accepted a part-time appointment to the Harvard Divinity School, in an arrangement that allowed him to travel to Latin America and lecture across North America on speaking tours. Yet despite his growing fame and popularity at Harvard, Nouwen was unable to deny something: he was unhappy. In his book *In the Name of Jesus*, he wrote: "After twenty-five years of priesthood, I found myself praying poorly, living somewhat isolated from other people, and very much preoccupied with burning issues...I woke up one day with the realization that I was living in a very dark place and the term *burnout* was a convenient psychological translation for a spiritual death."

In response to this "burnout," Nouwen responded to an invitation to live with the L'Arche community at Trosly, France in 1985. Founded by the charismatic Frenchman Jean Vanier, L'Arche (after the French word for *ark*) is an international organization built up of small communities that welcome people with physical and mental disabilities. Vanier had said to Nouwen, "Perhaps our people could offer you a home."

After a year in Trosly, Henri accepted an invitation to serve as pastor of the L'Arche community near Toronto, Canada. Here Henri would spend the rest of his life; here he finally felt that he had found a home.

The disabled taught Nouwen, as no one had before, the value of experiencing God in the present moment, without worrying about the future or regretting the past. "Who better than severely mentally handicapped people to teach us this liberating truth?" wrote Nouwen in his book *Lifesigns*. "They do not read newspapers, watch television or discuss the possibility of future disasters. They do not dwell upon the future. Instead they say, 'Feed me, dress me, touch me, hold me....Kiss me, speak with me. It is good to be here together now.'"

Besides his work as pastor at L'Arche, much of Nouwen's time during his early years there was spent caring for a young man named Adam Arnett, who needed help with his simple morning routine. For Nouwen, this kind of work was the opposite of the busy life of the lecture-circuit priest. It served as the basis for one of his most powerful books, *Adam: God's Beloved*. Another popular book, this one a meditation on forgiveness and reconciliation, *The Return of the Prodigal Son*, was also written during his years at L'Arche.

Renewed by his ministry at L'Arche, Nouwen continued his busy life of lecturing and writing. Wherever he lectured, though, he invited a disabled person from his community to accompany him. Still, the time at L'Arche did not solve all of his spiritual and emotional problems. "Even after he entered L'Arche," writes Michael O'Laughlin, "he was still restless, uncertain and, occasionally, even unable to cope." While in Toronto he also began an intense friendship with another man, an assistant at L'Arche, which developed into an infatuation on Nouwen's part. The friendship finally broke down, a source of deep suffering for Nouwen. In the wake of this turmoil, Nouwen left L'Arche for a time to deal with this pain and was eventually able to return. (In later years, the friendship was restored.) In 1996, on the way to Russia to film a documentary about Rembrandt's painting of the Prodigal Son, Nouwen suffered a heart attack in Holland. He died on September 21, 1996, at the age of 64, and was buried near his home: the L'Arche community in Toronto.

Though I've since read quite a few books by Henri Nouwen, I always seem to return to *The Genesee Diary*, which imprinted itself on my soul early in my spiritual journey. It's a simple book: the plain-spoken journal of the author's seven months with the Trappist abbey at Genesee, in Western New York in 1974. Nouwen, as I had mentioned, had gone to the abbey for an opportunity to pray and reassess the state of his hectic life. Like many of us, Nouwen felt that his life was often too busy for real communion with God. His course load at Yale, speaking engagements, and writing projects prevented Nouwen, who craved the attention and affirmation that each new assignment brought, from living more contemplatively. So he went to Genesee.

The Genesee Diary is a beautifully written book, and its main appeal for me lay in its luminous descriptions of the monastic life. Nouwen describes the joys of simple manual labor (much of his time is taken up with moving rocks from a river bed to their eventual place as part of a new chapel), the quirks and oddities of the Trappist community (he speaks both honestly and affectionately about the monks with whom he lives), and the surprising ways in which God speaks to the contemplative. In one of my favorite passages, Nouwen details almost the same type of joy that Merton often described when contemplating the natural world, a joy that, though solitary, calls forth a desire to be with others:

> A mysterious veil covered the fields just harvested, and the gentle hills of New York State seemed grateful for the moist air and showed themselves in a new beauty. I felt happy and grateful and kept thinking an old thought: I wished that all my friends who I love so much could see and feel what I see and feel today. But I know they never will. On this earth the experience of great beauty always remains mysteriously linked with the experience of great loneliness. This reminds me again that there is still a beauty I have not seen yet: the beauty that does not create loneliness but unity.

Nouwen does find God during his seven months at the Abbey of the Genesee, and begins to see glimpses of his true self, especially as revealed in the silences of prayer and in his relationships with the other monks. Yet he also concludes, somewhat ruefully, that he cannot escape from himself. The same problems he faced on the "outside"—that is, his need to be needed by others, his need to be seen as useful, his need to write and publish— follow him into the monastery and remain at the end of his stay.

Still, Nouwen's time at Genesee changes him in some important ways. He feels a deeper union with God in his prayer and, ironically, feels closer to the world he has left: seeing it with some distance enables him to feel more compassion toward it.

What I also found attractive in *The Genesee Diary* was Nouwen's brutal honesty and his overwhelming desire for the contemplative life, two things that support one another. Nouwen is, for example, almost unbelievably honest about his need for popularity, for fame, and for attention. At the same time, he writes feelingly about how something as simple as finding an unwanted stone among a pile of raisins about to be baked into the monastery's bread can be a contemplative experience, even an epiphany. Here, honesty and contemplation exist together, much as in the best of Merton, especially his journals.

I don't think that you *can* be a true contemplative without being utterly honest before yourself and God. I don't think you can be honest with yourself without being a contemplative in some way. One supports the other. Honesty before God and others deepens your relationship with God, and therefore your prayer. Likewise, a deepening intimacy with God frees you to be honest with yourself and with others.

When it comes to Thomas Merton and Henri Nouwen, it's not so much their formal essays on the contemplative life, or the priesthood, or religious life, or the church, or social justice, or peacemaking that I most admire, as much as it is their writings on their own *lives:* their journals and their autobiographical writings. This is the draw for many of their contemporary admirers, too. *The Seven Storey Mountain,* after all, is by far Merton's best-known work. Likewise, Nouwen's most popular books are reflections on his own experiences: whether working in Latin America in *¡Gracias!*, pondering the mystery of forgiveness as it relates to his family in *The Return of the Prodigal Son*, or meditating on the meaning of his work with disabled persons in *Adam*.

But what is it about how Merton and Nouwen wrote about their lives that attracts so many readers? Let me suggest four things.

First, the two are nearly always honest about their daily lives. The most compelling passages in their writings come when they are being candid about both the joys *and* struggles of their daily lives. Nouwen talking both about his joy at caring for Adam while living at the L'Arche community in Canada, and also about how frustrated he is that so few people are writing to him when he's at the Abbey of the Genesee. Merton describing how beautiful the trees are outside his little hermitage at the abbey, and also how angry he is at his abbot, or his brother Trappists, or his critics, or his superiors in France, or the Vatican. Or his abbot again. (Thomas Merton's abbot surely deserves his place in heaven for bearing the brunt of Merton's frequent bursts of anger and disappointment!)

Second, both Nouwen and Merton are flawed and sometimes sinful men who are not afraid to admit it. Both struggle, for example, with an overweening pride. Both of them can be, according to their own writings, incredibly difficult to get along with. They are both desperate for attention. Here is Nouwen dilating on some of these themes in *The Genesee Diary*, written in 1974. Like Merton, as soon as he gets what he wants and it doesn't work out, he grows angry or sullen:

> I know too well how hard it is to live without being needed, being wanted, being asked, being known, being admired,

being praised. Just a few years ago I retired from my teaching job in Holland and lived for a year as a student in a
rented room in the city. I had expected to be free at last to
study and do many of the things I couldn't do when I was
busy and so much in demand. But what happened?
Without a job I was soon forgotten. People I had hoped
would come and visit me didn't come; friends I expected to
invite me remained silent; fellow priests whom I thought
would ask me to assist them in their Sunday liturgy or to
preach once in a while didn't need me; and my surround-
ings had pretty well responded as if I were no longer around.
The irony was that I always wanted to be alone to work, but
when I was finally left alone, I couldn't work and started to
become more morose, angry, sour, hateful, bitter and com-
plaining.

That painful summary of disappointments and the concluding
catalogue of sins are heartfelt and real. "Hateful" is a strong
word. This is not false humility.

Neither is this, from Merton's journals, October,
1960, written right before he moves into the hermitage. As usual,
he's ticked off at his abbot:

It is exceptionally frustrating to have such a beautiful place
as this one is getting to be—tucked away among the pines—
and to have to stay away from it. Along with this, the con-
viction that the abbot has no interest in how I might feel
about this, is sure that my desires are absurd, and even fears
them. But in that case why did he do something that would
manifestly encourage them? I did not really ask for this, for
rather I showed a great deal of hesitation and gave him five
or six chances to reverse his decision and call the whole
thing off. This by now he will have completely forgotten.
Meanwhile I have a hard time appearing cheerful and socia-
ble. I can't say I've tried too hard, either. Complete disgust
with the stupid mentality we cultivate in our monasteries.

Deliberate cult of frustration and nonsense. Professional
absurdity. Isn't life absurd enough already without adding to
it our own fantastic frustrations and stupidities?

In their autobiographical writings, Merton and
Nouwen reveal themselves to be impatient, petty, neurotic, selfish, suspicious, testy, and sometimes even mean. But again, they
are honest about their sinfulness. This candor eventually allows
them to recognize the hand of God, and the invitation to greater
trust and intimacy with the Lord.

As an aside, this revelation of their flaws attracts as
much as it repels some readers. For me, it is attractive. It helps me
to feel closer to them and see more clearly how they grew spiri-
tually and, likewise, how I am invited to grow as they did, even
with my faults. In his book *The Return of the Prodigal Son*, for
example, Nouwen's extended discussion of why he feels like the
elder son in the Gospel parable—with his resentfulness of those
who have lived the high life, his anger at always having to be the
good son, and his constant desire for forgiveness—is deeply moving. That mode of writing calls forth the same emotions as when
someone reveals an intimate or painful part of his or her life. For
me it is a great gift in the order of grace, because it becomes very
clear at that moment how much God loves that person.

For other readers, the confessional style is a familiar
one, since it fits well into the open, self-confessional mode of many
popular memoirs today, as well as the open, self-confessional
memoirs that are the mainstays of classic Christian literature: the
autobiographies of Saint Augustine, Saint Teresa of Ávila, Saint
Ignatius Loyola, C. S. Lewis, and so on. The flawed, wounded
writer is appealing.

For still others, however, their flaws are themselves
off-putting, distancing rather than attracting readers. Many

readers are not interested in spending time with an author they don't like.

In the book club I help run at a local Jesuit church, we have read *The Genesee Diary* and *Return of the Prodigal Son*, as well as *The Seven Storey Mountain*, which we read over a period of two months. And there were just as many people who admired Nouwen's and Merton's openness as were repelled by what many saw as their self-centeredness. In the middle of a discussion about *The Seven Storey Mountain*, one elderly woman piped up and said how much she disliked Merton. She couldn't *stand* him. Too triumphalistic about Catholicism. Too dismissive of other Christian denominations. Too chauvinistic about women. Most of all, too self-centered. She said, "You know, you could read pages and pages of his autobiography around the period of the early 1940s and have no clue that there was a war going on." I had to admit that it was a fair critique.

Third, both Merton and Nouwen are always seeking. Nouwen's life, which can be traced even by the newcomer to his work through his books, moves from place to place to place. Nouwen never seems entirely satisfied until he comes to live at the L'Arche community. But even then, there are doubts and dissatisfactions. And Merton, of course, was forever questioning his place in the monastery, almost as soon as he took vows. Should I stay? Should I go? Should I join another religious order? Early in his monastic journals, you'll read: Well, my confessor says I should stay. So that's final: I'll stay. But a few months later he writes: Well, maybe not, maybe my confessor is wrong, maybe I should go.

This restlessness, not a bad thing in itself, is more problematic for a monk who takes a vow of stability, and this tension would continue until the end of Merton's life. Henri Nouwen manifests something of the same restlessness throughout *The Genesee Diary*. Should I live a more contemplative life? Okay, I should. No, I shouldn't give up my writing and speaking, since people profit by it. Okay, I *won't* give it up.

The two were always seekers, seeking a way to live out their vocations.

Fourth, both Merton and Nouwen struggled with the demands of chastity. This aspect of their lives is especially interesting to me as a celibate priest. Merton never seems, at least to me, to have had a healthy relationship with a woman until he met the young nurse Marge during a stay in a hospital in the 1960s, and even then his relationship was unhealthy since he was explicitly breaking his vows and, for a time, deceiving his Trappist brothers.

A striking image of Merton at that time of his affair with Marge is his asking visitors to his hermitage to bring fistfuls of quarters so he could leave the grounds of the monastery to make phone calls. It reminded me of something my novice director once told me: when you break one of your vows in a very big way, you are usually breaking the other two as well. So there is Merton, breaking his vow of chastity, as well as his vows of poverty and obedience.

Yet during this tempestuous period, Merton finally experienced the kind of deep romantic love that had eluded him his whole life. And he finally met a *real* woman he could love, and not some mythopoetic image of Proverb or Sophia or Wisdom or a theological construct of the Blessed Mother, which had been his typical way of relating to women as a monk—that is, primarily through his prayer and meditation. Throughout his whole life, though, Merton struggled to love honestly, openly, and chastely.

Nouwen, on the other hand, according to most accounts, was a gay man, and he struggled with this, as many celibate gay priests have done and still do. Michael Ford's excellent biography *Wounded Prophet: A Portrait of Henri J. M. Nouwen* speaks at length about this in a chapter entitled "New Directions," quoting friends in whom Nouwen confided this aspect of his personality. Though celibate, toward the end of his life, as I noted, he became infatuated and fell in love with another man at a L'Arche community, and he struggled with that, too. Perhaps because of formal restrictions or embarrassment or prudence or all three, he seems to have decided *not* to write publicly about this part of his life.

For myself, I think this represents something of a loss for his readers. Thomas Merton's honest journal entries about falling in love and then reaffirming his commitment to his religious vows are among his most powerful writings, and help us to reflect more deeply on celibacy, chastity, fidelity, love, intimacy, and, in the end, on faith. Of course, Merton's journals on this period emerged many years after his death. Still, it would be illuminating to read Nouwen's reflections on similar topics in light of his own sexuality.

Overall, both Merton and Nouwen tried, throughout their lives, to be loving men living their vows of chastity. Loving men of integrity. Like all priests, and like all people, they did this well at times and poorly at other times.

But you cannot talk about chastity without talking about friendships. Both Merton and Nouwen had a great capacity for friendships and a talent for maintaining a wide circle of friends, something that is absolutely essential for a life of chastity. Interestingly, though Merton craved friendship as much as anyone does, it's fair to say that he seems to have *needed* his friends somewhat less than Nouwen did.

In a short book of essays entitled *Encounters with Merton*, Nouwen writes almost longingly of Merton's ability to do this. Thomas Merton, he wrote, "loved his friends, but didn't use them, he was intensely thankful for everything he received from them, but he didn't attach himself to them. More and more he learned to see his friends as signposts to God." Here Nouwen is admiring an aspect of Merton's life that occasionally seems to have eluded him: detachment.

Indeed, it should be emphasized that, for all their similarities, Thomas Merton and Henri Nouwen were different men. In Michael Ford's book *Wounded Prophet*, the Trappist monk and former abbot of the Genesee, John Eudes Bamberger, who knew both Merton and Nouwen, drew some clear distinctions between the two. At the most basic level, Nouwen was engaged in an active life of the educator and lecturer, while Merton led the contemplative life of the monk. Nouwen, according to Bamberger, was essentially a teacher and communicator who reached a more popular level of readers, whereas Merton, the literary man, wrote for a more specific group. Finally, Merton was an "extraordinarily intelligent" person, whereas Nouwen's experiences were closer to the experiences of the "average, intelligent, devoted and serious person." Father Bamberger concludes: "Anybody who thinks Nouwen was the Merton of his generation didn't know Henri or didn't know Merton."

Still, Merton and Nouwen share many qualities that make them appealing to contemporary believers. First, they always tried to be honest. Second, they were not afraid to admit their sinfulness. Third, they were open-hearted seekers. And fourth, they tried to love.

In other words, they were *human*; they mirror us all. Thus we can easily identify with them. They were flawed persons who nevertheless loved God and were loved by God. They were "loved sinners," to use a phrase from Ignatian spirituality.

A wonderful thing about reading the lives of these two men in particular is that you can stand back and say: "Yes, I see the flaws and the problems and the sinfulness, but these were still very holy men." Perhaps that is the way that God sees all of us: holy even with our limitations and faults. And that is a very encouraging thought.

In their lives and in their writings, both Merton and Nouwen sought to be themselves before God. This was perhaps their most basic quest, and this is where they are excellent examples for contemporary Christians. Because for Merton and Nouwen, the lifelong process of self-examination and self-criticism and self-revelation had a point; it was not simply a narcissistic quest for self-knowledge. Rather, it was a discipline undertaken to allow them to become more loving and more centered on God. For both men, the long process of self-understanding enabled them to grow in freedom and to become more authentically themselves. To use some of their favorite terminology, it enabled Merton to become his "true self." And it enabled Nouwen to become "God's beloved."

"For me to be a saint means to be myself," wrote Merton in *New Seeds of Contemplation*. As I have said, there are few more liberating lines in contemporary Christian spirituality.

And few people have written about our personal paths to sanctity as beautifully as Thomas Merton and Henri Nouwen. God has made each of us uniquely ourselves, and holiness consists of discovering the true self, the person we are before God, accepting that person, and becoming a saint in the process.

Chapter Six

The Truest Self

Before I talked about Henri Nouwen, I probably should have mentioned another person I met as a novice: Jesus of Nazareth.

It is a tremendous understatement to say that I spent a lot of time in the novitiate thinking about Jesus. During daily Masses (the first time I had even *been* to a daily Mass was as a Jesuit) the novices heard the Gospel stories of the life, death, and resurrection of Jesus Christ. We were also encouraged to develop a "personal relationship" with Jesus in our prayer, by meditating on his words and deeds and imagining ourselves in some of the Gospel scenes with him. During meetings with the novice director and our spiritual director, we were regularly asked about our images and impressions about Jesus. (A not-too-surprising question for members of a group whose formal name is "The Society of Jesus.")

There were also dozens of books in the novitiate library that offered background material on Jesus, and I soon found myself drawn to studies on the "historical Jesus" or the "Jesus of history," which detailed what historians and archaeologists had discovered about the life of Jesus of Nazareth and the world of first-century Palestine. The first book I read on the topic was a short volume entitled *Jesus Before Christianity*, by the Dominican priest Albert Nolan, which provided a historical context for what was going on in all those Gospel stories I was hearing about during Mass.

The main event of the Jesuit novitiate was a one-month-long silent retreat based on the famous Spiritual Exercises of Saint Ignatius Loyola. During the Spiritual Exercises, the retreatant meditates on the entire life of Jesus: his birth, his young adulthood, his preaching and miracles, and his crucifixion, death, and resurrection. With four or five hours of prayer daily, this was certainly the most intensive period we would spend meditating on the story of Jesus of Nazareth.

In short, I thought about Jesus a lot.

For me, the most interesting question about Jesus concerned what theologians call his "self-knowledge." For example, how did Jesus see himself? How did he understand his ministry? Did he know that he was the Son of God?

As I said at the beginning of the book, I am no theologian or academic or scholar. So I won't be proposing any new theological theories here. Besides, when it comes to Jesus, I think the Christian tradition says it best: he was both fully human and fully divine. But this famous definition, which itself raises more questions than it answers, hardly settles the question of how Jesus thought of himself. And the more you meditate on the issue, the more you see how that question turns on how Jesus understood *his* true self.

Of course anything we say is speculative. During my theology studies, one student asked our New Testament professor about Jesus' self-knowledge. I remember the fellow stood up to ask a series of long and impassioned questions: When Jesus thought about himself, asked the student, did he know he was divine? When he prayed, how did he relate to God the Father? How did he know what he was supposed to do? Did he know that he was the Messiah? What did he think about the miracles he performed? Overall, what was his inner life like? My professor, a distinguished scholar and dedicated priest, listened carefully, paused for a moment and said, "We have no idea."

Still, it's a fascinating question, and one that every serious Christian needs to grapple with. It comes up, for example, when you think about the crucifixion. (If Jesus was divine, did he know that he would rise from the dead, and did this lessen his suffering on the cross?) And it comes up when you think about his relationship with his disciples. Recently, as I mentioned, I worked with an acting company on a play about Jesus and Judas. During one rehearsal, the question of Jesus' two "natures" (human and divine) was raised by one of the actors. Seated on the bare floor of the theater, in the middle of a scene opposite Judas Iscariot, the fellow playing Jesus said, "I'm not sure how I am supposed to be relating to Judas. Am I divine and do I know everything about him? Or am I still a man?"

A great question.

While it's true that we know little about the inner life of Jesus, there are some things that we can know. First of all, as a first-century Galilean Jew, he wouldn't have used the same language that we use today to describe himself. As the theologian Elizabeth Johnson says in her book *Consider Jesus*, "Obviously Jesus did not wake up in the morning saying, 'I am the Son of God with a truly human nature and a truly divine nature that comes together in one hypostasis.' I do not know what he said in the morning, but we can be virtually certain that it was not that!"

If this was the case, how *did* Jesus understand his true self?

We have to begin with the foundational Christian belief that Jesus was fully human and fully divine. And while we shouldn't lose sight of either "nature," it's the human part that gets forgotten more often. Even devout Christians tend to neglect his real humanity—which means not knowing the future, slowly figuring out one's calling, and living by faith. What follows, then, is a sort of imaginative exercise to explore the human way in which Jesus of Nazareth might have grown into his true self. In other words, here's how I like to think about it.

If we're talking about the self-knowledge of Jesus, or how Jesus came to understand his true self, we should begin in his early adolescence, the time when most people first start thinking about who they are and who they want to be. For a boy in first-century Palestine, this might have started as early as age thirteen, which in later Jewish life became the traditional time of coming of age marked by the *bar mitzvah*.

Unfortunately, the Gospel writers say nothing about the life of Jesus between the time he is discovered teaching in the Temple, at age twelve, and the beginning of his public ministry, around age thirty. "And Jesus increased in wisdom and in years, and in divine and human favor," is all the Gospel of Luke says (2:52). In other words, there is an eighteen-year gap in our knowledge about the life of Jesus. Yet this period, often called the "hidden life," was undoubtedly crucial in the growing self-awareness and maturation of Jesus.

What might this time have been like for Jesus? It's reasonable to think that as Mary and Joseph meditated on the unusual birth and early childhood of their son, they may have come to believe that he was destined for a unique vocation. So perhaps some of their own conclusions and reflections were passed on to Jesus. At the same time, their son probably spent much of his time preparing for what he may have imagined would be his lifelong occupation: a carpenter, or what we might also call a craftsman or construction worker. (Significantly, the Gospels refer to Jesus more frequently as "the carpenter" rather than "the rabbi.") And, as far as his true self goes, it is also not unreasonable to think that the virtues that Jesus acquired as a carpenter (patience, hard work, honesty, and so on) would serve him well in his later ministry. In conversations with Mary and Joseph, and in his daily work in Nazareth, Jesus was being prepared by God for his eventual work, much as God can use our own backgrounds and talents for the good.

Since one can speculate freely, I like to think of his young adulthood as the time during which Jesus first started to wonder if he was meant for some special purpose. Perhaps this came from his own prayer, or from the way he felt when he read certain Scripture passages, especially the prophetic writings, like the Book of Isaiah. Perhaps when he saw friends in Nazareth who were sick, he felt his heart moved with pity. Perhaps when he saw the religious leaders laying heavy burdens on the people, he sensed the unfairness of life and how far this was from what God wanted. Perhaps, then, he started to believe that his life should be about alleviating suffering. Perhaps over time he felt within himself a desire that became progressively clearer: to preach the word of God and somehow to lessen the suffering of those around him. Perhaps, as he looked at Nazareth and the surrounding Jewish towns, he wondered whether he didn't have some great part to play in the liberation of his people. Overall, I like to think of Jesus as a pensive young man, who thought hard about the person God intended him to be.

Even when he reached the age of thirty, however, Jesus may still have been a bit unclear about things. After all, many of us are still unclear about things at that age, and Jesus had a lot to be unclear about! Indeed, at the very beginning of his public ministry, Jesus seems unsure about what he's supposed to do. You could make a case that when Jesus went to the Jordan River to be baptized, it was because, like so many people, he was attracted to the message of John the Baptist. That is, he may have gone to see what John's message was all about and whether it would help him understand what he was meant to do. Indeed, his baptism by John seems to be confusing even for some of the Gospel writers. After all, why would Jesus have to be baptized with a "baptism of repentance for the forgiveness of sins," as the Gospel of Mark (1:4) describes it? If anything, shouldn't the Son of God be doing the baptizing himself? In his Gospel, Matthew feels obliged to provide an explanation (albeit a vague one) which he places in Jesus' lips: "Let it be so now; for it is proper for us in this way to fulfill all righteousness" (3:15).

Whatever the reasons that drew Jesus to the banks of the Jordan River, something happened at his baptism that was so astounding (the Gospels describe it as the heavens opening and a voice being heard) that it convinces Jesus that he has a uniquely important mission. And so he is driven into the desert to continue his process of prayer and discernment.

Clearly Jesus was sorely tested in the desert. Whether you believe Satan appeared in some physical way to do the testing personally or whether Jesus experienced these tests, or temptations, within himself seems beside the point to my mind. But the great Scripture scholar William Barclay suggests that this episode was most likely passed along to the disciples by Jesus himself, and so it needs to be taken very seriously.

The testing in the desert may be the easiest part of Jesus' life to understand. Jesus, now thinking intently about his mission, was subject to the same temptations that all of us are: for power, for security, for easy answers. But he rejects these temptations and returns to Galilee to begin his ministry.

Those few weeks in the life of Jesus, as he turns away from power, security, and easy answers, are critical for any reflection in the search for the true self. You could see it as a fundamental rejection of the temptation to become the "false self." For underlying all the impulses that Jesus experienced in the desert was a temptation to do things in a way that would contradict who he was called to be. The temptations said to him: "Don't become who you were called to be. Be someone who is more in line with selfish wants, with what society demands, with what will give superficial success and pleasure. Be someone who fits in, who never poses a threat to the status quo. Be someone who craves only respect. Be your false self."

But Jesus may have also faced tests that were more subtle than that. For example, Jesus may have been tempted to assume worldly power as a means to help people. After all, why *not* be the powerful and influential person if that power and influence can aid others? Gradually, Jesus realizes that God is calling him to a very different kind of power.

In facing down these temptations in the desert, in turning away from a self-centered life and a life of worldly power, Jesus rejects his false self and embraces his true self.

But even after his stay in the desert, there still seems a lingering reticence in Jesus to embrace his mission. For what is traditionally considered as his first miracle seems a distinctly reluctant one. There he is at the wedding feast at Cana when the wine runs out (John 2:1–11). (In the play I mentioned, Judas describes the host as "some lowly distant relative too cheap to provide enough booze for his own wedding.") When his mother points this out to him, in effect, suggesting that he do something, Jesus says, somewhat caustically, "Woman, what concern is that to you and to me?" (2:4). In other words, what does this have to do with me? I'm not the person you want! I'm not yet the person I am called to be! Here Jesus may still be grappling with his mission, with his vocation, and with his true self.

In response, his mother gives him the freedom to do what he wants. "Do whatever he tells you," she says placidly to the servants (2:5). Interestingly, Mary may have understood his mission earlier than Jesus did, perhaps because she had had a longer time to think about it.

Somehow Jesus now understands what is required of him. Confident now, he tells the steward to fill large earthen jars with water and serve the guests. But it is not water that comes out of the jars, it is wine. It is his first miracle.

I have always wondered if Jesus himself wasn't surprised by his first miracle. In his journey toward self-knowledge, if there were ever a time when he might have been surprised, it is in Cana.

In my own life, I am consistently surprised by the results of my own ministry. Needless to say, I don't change water into wine, but I say just a few words to someone in confession that unlock emotions and feelings that have long been hidden away. I casually mention a Gospel passage in spiritual direction that turns out to be precisely the right one for someone to experience healing or hope. After a chance remark during a homily, someone approaches me saying through tears that this was just what she needed to hear.

Just recently, I was present at the precise moment when someone found out some very bad news and I was able to spend time with him in a small, private room that had just become available in a busy setting. After an intense conversation, and some tears, we both stood up to leave. Just then a person abruptly entered the room and told us that she needed it. Had we been just a few minutes earlier, or a few minutes later, my friend and I would not have had the chance or the time or the space to meet. It seemed God had cleared a space for that conversation just when my friend needed it.

The fruits of one's ministry and one's life are often astonishing, and the hand of God can be seen as clear as day, even when the results are simple ones. How much more surprising, then, might the miracle at Cana have been for Jesus!

At the same time, the miracle at Cana seems to have strengthened Jesus' understanding of his mission and emboldened him to trust even more in God, to trust even more in his judgment and discernment, and to trust in his ability to do miraculous things in the name of God. It may have helped Jesus to see the value of his true self, and understand the mission that his Father had sent him for: to be the revealer and revelation of God.

This is also the case in our own lives. The more we live out our true selves, and the more we become the person whom God intended, the more we see the spectacular effects of a well-lived vocation. The father who fully embraces his vocation as a father becomes a better father, and his children receive even more love. The mother becomes a better mother. The doctor becomes a better doctor. The friend becomes a better friend. And the Christian becomes a better Christian.

As the Gospel stories continue, it is easy to see Jesus growing in confidence in his mission and in his identity. His miracles are a measure of his confidence in himself and in his mission, which flows from his relationship with his Father. In other passages, this assurance virtually leaps off the page, as in a story that is told in the Gospels of Matthew, Mark, and Luke.

"Lord, if you choose," says a leper, "you can make me clean."

"I do choose," says Jesus, full of confidence. "Be made clean!"

Throughout his ministry, Jesus continues to grow in his awareness of his mission and his true self.

Toward the end of his earthly ministry, Jesus is clearly able to see what needs to be done. He has by this point more fully embraced his identity and his ministry. But there is one last test: his time in the Garden of Gethsemane immediately before the beginning of his Passion. Near the end of his life, he struggles with a complete embrace of his mission. "If it is possible, let this cup pass from me," he says, hoping that perhaps suffering is not what God intends (Matt 26:39).

But somehow he realizes, through prayer and reflection, that his impending suffering, whatever it would be, is what God is asking of him at this moment. He realizes that it is part of the reality of his life. And it is here, it seems to me, that in accepting the cup of suffering, Jesus fully and decisively accepts his identity. Part of his life and vocation includes suffering, as do all of our lives and vocations. In the Garden, Jesus accepts this essential human truth.

Jesus is then completely free. He is not disturbed when he is arrested in the Garden, having just been betrayed by one of his closest friends. In response to Peter's striking one of the high priest's guards, Jesus calmly heals the man and points the disciples to a peaceful acceptance of his path. In the face of Pilate's questioning, he refuses to allow himself even the chance to defend himself. He is, in fact, largely silent during the Passion. And as he moves toward death, carrying his cross, he is firm in his acceptance of his true self, a self whose life includes suffering and death. His crucifixion becomes a deeply human act, not only because dying is perhaps the most human thing he does, but because it is an outgrowth of his great "yes" to the totality of his true self.

I've always wondered if Jesus knew for certain that he would be raised from the dead. Now, I may be completely wrong, but I think that while Jesus lived his life in perfect faith, and trusted that something wonderful would come from his acceptance of his mission and his obedience to his Father—as it always had in the past—he did not know precisely what this would mean.

There are indications of this in the Gospels. Even while he hung on the cross, though freely giving himself to his mission, he cried out in pain and confusion, "My God, my God, why have you forsaken me?" (Matt 27:46).

For me, this possible ignorance of his own future makes his acceptance of the reality of his human life more meaningful. He trusted God so completely that he knew that by becoming his true self, even in the midst of unimaginable suffering, he would somehow bring new life to others. And perhaps even Jesus didn't know what this new life would be, until the morning of that first Easter, when his true self was finally revealed in all its splendor and glory. It's wonderful to think that even *he* was surprised at the new life given him by God. Perhaps it was only then that in Elizabeth Johnson's beautiful phrase, "his ultimate identity burst upon him with all clarity."

The life of Christ is the central metaphor for the Christian life. And the way that Jesus understood who he was, what he was meant to do, and how he was meant to do it, is a metaphor for the Christian journey to the true self. All of us are called to meditate deeply on our own true selves, to embrace the reality of our vocations, and to let God transform our true selves into sources of new life for others. It's a long route, a lifetime journey, but we are not alone. We have the support of the rest of the community, we have the Holy Spirit inspiring us, we have the love of God the Father, and we have the companionship of the truest self of all, Jesus Christ.

*The past
does not
belong to me;

the future
is not mine;

with all my soul
I try to make use o[f]
the present momen[t]*

ant spiritual insight I've learned
: Jesuits is that God calls each of us
"For me to be a saint means for me
erton. (I promise that's the last time
you've memorized it by now!) As a
ing true to the person God created.
means being your true self. And
besides the life of Jesus of Nazareth, the best illustration of this can be found in the lives of the saints.

I know that many readers might groan (inwardly or outwardly) when they hear this. Because, unfortunately, for many people the lives of the saints are considered overly pious and largely irrelevant legends. It can seem almost impossible to relate to people known primarily as marble statues or stained-glass windows. You look at a statue of, say, Saint Thérèse of Lisieux, the "Little Flower," in her Carmelite habit, holding a bouquet of roses and looking heavenward, and it's not hard to think, "What does *that* have to do with my life?"

But it's important to remember that the saints were human beings, which means that they sinned (frequently), doubted (sometimes), and wondered whether they were doing the right thing (more often than you would think). As anyone does, the saints struggled with casting off the vestiges of their false selves and becoming who God wanted them to be.

As an aside, I'm using the term "saints" in its broadest possible meaning: not simply for those who have been "canonized" by the church (that is, officially declared saints and worthy of public veneration), but also for those holy men and women who may not yet be officially recognized as such. But the use of the term in that way has a distinguished background. Saint Paul, for example, employed the same word to refer to his early Christian companions. "To the saints who are in Ephesus," begins one letter (Eph 1:1). "To the church of God that is in Corinth," he writes in another, "including all the saints throughout Achaia..." (2 Cor 1:1).

At some point in their lives, each saint realized that God was calling them to be faithful in a particular way. Each saint was placed in a different situation and time. Each had a different personality and dealt with life differently. And each related to God a little differently. Just think of the astonishing variety of saints. And I don't mean simply when they lived, what they did, where they were from, or what languages they spoke. I mean something more basic: who they were and how they lived out their call to holiness.

Some examples: Though both of their lives were rooted and grounded in God, Thomas Merton's approach to life resembled very little that of Saint Aloysius Gonzaga, a young Jesuit who lived in sixteenth-century Rome. Merton was forever questioning his vow of stability, his place in the monastery, and his vocation as a Trappist, until the end of his life. Aloysius Gonzaga, on the other hand, the scion of a noble family, seemed always to have known precisely what he wanted to do—that is, become a Jesuit—from childhood. At a young age, Aloysius had to battle both his father and his brother to convince them to allow him to enter the Jesuit novitiate. Merton only had to battle himself. Merton's vocation seemed always to waver. Aloysius's never did.

Or consider Saint Thérèse of Lisieux, the French Carmelite, and Dorothy Day, the American apostle of social justice and founder of the Catholic Worker movement. Thérèse realized that God had called her to spend life cloistered behind the walls of the convent, while Dorothy Day understood that her invitation was to spend a life on the "outside," working among the poor in the big cities. Each grasped this. But both appreciated ways of sanctity that diverged from their own. Thérèse, for instance, admired the Catholic missionaries working in Vietnam. And Dorothy Day admired Thérèse.

Blessed Pope John XXIII meditates on this idea in his book *Journal of a Soul*, the compendium of autobiographical writings that he kept from seminary until almost the time of his death. In January 1907, he wrote that we must incorporate the "substance" of the saint's lives into our own. "I am not Saint Aloysius, nor must I seek holiness in his particular way." None of us, he continued, are meant to be a "dry, bloodless representation of a model, however perfect." Rather, wrote John, we are meant to follow the examples of the saints and apply them to our own lives.

"If Saint Aloysius had been as I am," he concluded, "he would have been holy in a different way."

Holy in a different way. Everyone's true self is a unique creation of God's, and the way to sanctity is to become the unique self that God wishes us to be.

The earliest example of the variety of ways to be Christian is found in the call of the First Disciples. Scripture scholar William Barclay in his Daily Study Bible series offered some provocative insights on why Jesus of Nazareth might have chosen fishermen among his first disciples. Good fishermen are patient, they are brave, they are persevering, they know how to fit the bait to the fish, they know how to stay out of sight, and so on. All good qualities for a disciple, too.

The simple fishermen of Galilee were most likely straightforward men, too, blunt and practical and unwilling to put up with any nonsense. The play I mentioned, *The Last Days of Judas Iscariot*, includes a moving monologue from Saint Peter, who remembers his brother Andrew as talking incessantly about the coming of the Messiah. The practical fisherman will have none of this crazy daydreaming.

"Look, fellas," says Peter, "unless your Messiah is gonna come down right now and help us catch some damn fish, then y'all need to shut the heck up and put your undivided focus on these damn nets."

Later in his monologue, Peter recalls meeting Jesus, who asks him to return to sea after an unsuccessful night of fishing. When Jesus asks him to cast out his nets again, Peter scoffs, but does so anyway. And then Peter is given a taste of what life with Jesus would mean: "All I can say is that I'm a damn professional commercial fisherman," says Peter. "No one knew the sea and its tides better than me. There weren't no fish out there...but... that's because it turned out they was all in my net."

Jesus probably chose fishermen for the very qualities that this dramatized version of Peter demonstrated. But that explains the reasons for choosing only a few of the disciples, those four who were fishermen. What about everyone else? Why would Jesus call, say, a tax collector and a religious zealot, and, among his wider circle of disciples, notorious sinners?

One reason may have been that Jesus saw each disciple's ability to contribute something unique to the community. The unity of the church, both then and now, encompasses diversity. As Saint Paul wrote, "Now there are a variety of gifts, but the same Spirit....To each is given a manifestation of the Spirit for the common good....For just as the body is one and has many members, and all the members of the body, though many, are one body, so it is with Christ" (1 Cor 12:4, 7, 12). All of us bring something unique to the table, and, through our own gifts, we each manifest a personal way of holiness that enlivens the larger community. We help to build up the "Kingdom of God" in ways that others may not. Mother Teresa catches this insight in her most famous saying: "You can do something I cannot do. I can do something you cannot do. Together let us do something beautiful for God."

This diversity is a natural outgrowth of the role of simple human desire, whose place in the spiritual life is often overlooked. Put simply, the saints had different desires and those desires led them to serve God in different ways. Such desires affected not only what they did, but who they became, their true selves.

These natural inclinations are ways in which God accomplishes his work in various places and in a variety of modes. When I was studying theology, our Jesuit community had a small poster hanging in our living room that offered this little saying about four great founders of religious orders:

> *Bernardus valles,*
> *Colles Benedictus amavit,*
> *Oppida Franciscus,*
> *Magnas Ignatius urbes.*

That is:

Bernard loved the valleys,
Benedict the hills,
Francis the small towns
and Ignatius the great cities.

Each of these four saints found his home in a place suited to his likes and desires, and so was moved to accomplish his own particular task. Their individual desires shaped their vocations. Ignatius Loyola, for example, the founder of the Jesuits, would probably have felt his ambitious plans stymied in a small town. And Francis of Assisi, the apostle of the poor, would certainly have gone crazy trying to run a large religious order from a busy office in Rome!

God awakens our vocations primarily through our desires. A man and a woman, for example, come together in love out of desire and so discover their vocation as a married couple. Out of desire, a husband and wife create a child, and discover their vocation as parents in this way. Desire works in a similar way in the lives of the saints, drawing them to certain types of works, giving rise to special vocations and leading to particular styles of holiness. Henri Nouwen became a priest because he desired it. Thérèse of Lisieux entered the convent because she desired it. Dorothy Day entered the Catholic Church because she desired it. Ultimately, one's deepest desires lead to God and the fulfillment of God's desires for the world.

That insight lies behind one of my favorite passages in *The Seven Storey Mountain*. Shortly after his baptism, Thomas Merton is speaking with his good friend Bob Lax. Merton tells his friend he wants to be a good Catholic. "What you should

say," says his friend in reply, "is that you want to be a saint."
Merton tells the rest of the story:

> A saint? The thought struck me as a little weird. I said:
>   "How do you expect me to become a saint?"
>   "By wanting to," said Lax, simply…. "All that is necessary
> to be a saint is to want to be one. Don't you believe God will
> make you what He created you to be, if you consent to let
> Him do it? All you have to do is desire it."

The next day Merton speaks with his mentor, Mark
Van Doren, the esteemed professor of English at Columbia
University, and mentions his confusing conversation. Van
Doren's response is both direct and disarming.

> "Lax is going around telling everyone that all a man needs
> to be a saint is to want to become one."
>   "Of course," said Mark.

Following these individual desires and inclinations
led each of the saints to a distinctive type of holiness. As Thomas
Aquinas, the great thirteenth-century theologian said, grace builds
on nature. Ignatius Loyola ended a military career in sixteenth-
century Spain to follow God, while Joan of Arc began one in
fifteenth-century France. Dorothy Day founded a newspaper to
spread the Gospel, while Bernadette Soubirous, the famous
visionary of Lourdes, shrank in horror from the idea of her story
being publicized in the press. Thomas Aquinas spent his life sur-
rounded by books, while Francis of Assisi told his friars not to
own even *one* lest they become too proud. The multiplicity of
desires leads to a multiplicity of paths to God.

But there is a problem with this diversity; that is, the challenge in appreciating another person's path that is different from our own. While the saints grasped this, it can present more of an obstacle for the rest of us. If you're a naturally active person, you might wonder about the sedentary life of a contemplative ("All that prayer when there's so much to be *done*?"). If you're of a contemplative bent, you might question the frenetic life of the activist ("All that activity when all God wants is for you to be with God in *prayer*?"). You can easily imagine Saint Peter looking at Saint Paul and grumbling to himself, "I'm supposed to work with a former Pharisee?"

It can be especially difficult to accept another's unique way of discipleship if we are unsure of our own. Such misunderstanding can lead to disagreement and even strife within the Christian community. But it's helpful to remember that even the saints disagreed with one another—often strongly. Quarrels among the saints in fact have a venerable tradition in the Christian church, going all the way back to Peter and Paul. (Could you get any more venerable than that?) There is a more contemporary example in Paul Elie's book about American Catholicism, *The Life You Save May Be Your Own*, that wonderfully illustrates this.

Elie tells the story of Dorothy Day's visit to Georgia in 1957. Koinonia, an interracial farming cooperative, was made up of some sixty people, both black and white, and the surrounding townspeople were making things difficult for the integrated community. The barn had been set afire and the houses shot at. After a long bus ride from New York City, Dorothy arrived and was promptly shot at by angry neighbors for her troubles. On her return to New York she wrote a series of moving articles for *The Catholic Worker* about her sojourn in Georgia.

Today most observers would look at that story and say, "Another saintly act by Dorothy Day!" But another devout Catholic, the novelist Flannery O'Connor, who spent much of her life in Georgia writing sensitively on issues of race herself, saw otherwise. She found Dorothy's attitude prideful, as if Dorothy Day knew better than anyone in Georgia what needed to be done. As Paul Elie writes, Flannery O'Connor saw this as news of her own county delivered "by way of the Upper East Side."

O'Connor was even blunter in a letter to a friend: "It would have been all right if she hadn't had to stick in her plug for Their Way of Life for Everybody." Although she admired Dorothy Day, O'Connor wrote, "All of my thoughts on the subject are ugly and uncharitable — such as: that's a mighty long way to come and get shot at, etc."

In other words, not only did Dorothy Day and Flannery O'Connor have their own styles of holiness, they had, in this case, opposing ways of seeing the hand of God in the world and, consequently, a different understanding of what was required of them. They went about their discipleship in their own fashions: Dorothy Day through journalism and activism, Flannery O'Connor by writing novels and taking care of her aging mother (and her flock of peacocks, too).

So what holds things together in the midst of this diversity? What keeps the communion of saints in communion?

The unity in the lives of the Christian saints rests on their commitment to Jesus Christ. Much as in the case of the early disciples, who trusted the judgment of their teacher, God calls people quite different from ourselves for reasons that may remain mysterious to us. As a Jesuit I have frequently met people who sing the praises of another Jesuit whom I have written off as too quiet or too cerebral or too ornery to do any good. It's a reminder of the wisdom of the One who calls us together and sends us on mission.

Perhaps, in fact, all that kept the fractious disciples together was Jesus himself. Not so much his settling of disagreements, but their fundamental trust in him. They may have said to themselves, "Okay, Lord, I don't like that other fellow very much, and I don't really understand him, but if *you* say he's part of our group, that's good enough for me."

But here's an important point: even the saints and holy persons faced difficult and often painful challenges before realizing their own brand of holiness. Some struggled for a long time before they truly understood their own vocation. Thomas Merton, as I mentioned, spent years trying to cast off the "bandages" of his false self before he could begin living as his true self. Henri Nouwen did not find his place among the disabled at L'Arche, did not find his home, until the age of fifty-four.

Some of the saints faced seemingly insurmountable odds even *after* they embraced their vocations: Aloysius Gonzaga, though he was sure about his Jesuit vocation, had first to convince his father, a powerful nobleman, who initially threatened to have him flogged for wanting to join the Jesuits. The mother of Thomas Aquinas sent her other sons in pursuit of Thomas to prevent him from joining the Dominicans. Waylaying him on the road one day, they captured Thomas and forcibly returned him to his family, who had him imprisoned in the family castle for two years, hoping that he would change his mind. (He didn't.)

There are also a surprising number of stories from the lives of the saints that show that some of their deepest desires were frustrated. That is, they seemed prevented from becoming who *they* wanted to be. After her famous visions at the Grotto of Lourdes in 1858, Bernadette Soubirous, who had wanted to continue her old life as a shepherdess, was more or less pushed into a convent by her otherwise well-meaning pastor. (The idea that a future saint would want to be a shepherdess—and worse, possibly married—was anathema to the religious people of the day.) A few years later, in her Carmelite convent, Thérèse of Lisieux confessed her ardent desire for ordination to the priesthood in her book, *Story of a Soul:* "I feel in me the *vocation* of the priest," she wrote. This, of course, was something that would not occur in her lifetime. And Thomas Merton had to face the continual frustration of not having the opportunity for more solitude, until the end of his life, when he was granted permission to become a hermit on the grounds of the abbey.

In other words, finding one's true self can be a long, arduous, and even confusing journey.

Still, throughout these painful spiritual trials, these men and women continued to pray over the ways that God was calling them to be themselves, even in the midst the frustrations and roadblocks that life put in front of them. Not able to be a priest, Thérèse still grew in holiness. Not able to marry, Bernadette still grew in holiness. Not able to find a sense of stability, Nouwen still grew in holiness. Not able to have the solitude he craved, Merton still grew in holiness. In the midst of their disappointments, God still enabled them to move closer to their true selves.

At this point you still may be thinking, "Well, I'm not like *any* of the people just mentioned. I'm neither a social activist like Dorothy Day, nor a contemplative like Thomas Merton, nor a writer like Henri Nouwen, nor a founder of a religious order like Mother Teresa, nor a visionary leader like Francis of Assisi, and certainly not an *actual* visionary like Bernadette Soubirous. Holiness is beyond me. My true self is not meant for sanctity."

I disagree. I believe that sanctity is God's goal for all of us, our *telos*, our endpoint. As Mother Teresa said, "Holiness is not the luxury of a few. It is everyone's duty: yours and mine." That's pretty abstract, so let's make things more concrete.

Despite the recent emphasis on every person's call to holiness, many Christians, I would wager, still believe that sanctity is reserved only for people who are long dead, like Peter or Mary Magdalene, or the professionally religious person, like Henri Nouwen or Thérèse of Lisieux or Thomas Merton. Or those who die for their faith, like the early Christian martyrs. Or maybe, just maybe, the extraordinary layperson, like the parent who dedicates his or her entire life to caring for the poor, like Jean Vanier, the founder of the L'Arche movement. But the idea of the holy person *in everyday life* still strikes many people as strange.

Let's say that you're a young married woman with two little children, ages four and six. When the alarm clock jolts you awake in the early morning, you realize that you're still weary from the day before. As usual, your two children are already awake. One is crying her eyes out because she's had a bad dream. Your other child is already calling for a drink of water, and for his favorite stuffed animal, which he tossed out of his bed last night. And let's say that your husband is away on a business trip, and can't help you with the kids that morning. Let's also say that you have a job outside the home as well, and have to make breakfast and get the kids ready for school, before leaving for another hectic day at your office.

As you lie in bed for a few seconds, staring at the ceiling, you think about all the things you have to do for your family today, all of the things you have to do for your boss at the office, and none of the things you can do for yourself. You wonder how you'll be able to accomplish even half of what you need to do today. Sometimes, during these early-morning moments, you lament the fact that you don't have time for things like prayer or meditation. You wish you lived a holier life, a more *religious* life. Recently you read a magazine article about your favorite contemporary saint, Mother Teresa. You say to yourself, sadly, "I'll never be like her." But that's the problem. You're not *meant* to be Mother Teresa, you're meant to be *yourself.*

Here's where Merton's description of the true self and false self is particularly useful. As I have mentioned, the false self is the person that we present to the world, the one that we think will be pleasing to others: attractive, confident, successful. The true self, on the other hand, is the person that we are before God. Sanctity consists in discovering who that person is and striving to become that person.

In other words, the working mother is not *meant* to be Mother Teresa. She is meant to be a woman who loves her children, loves her husband, loves her friends and coworkers, and finds meaning in her own world. She is meant to experience the presence of God in her life and in the lives of the people with whom she lives and works. Sometimes this means doing big things with love, like raising children. And sometimes it means doing smaller things with love. (Thérèse of Lisieux called this the "Little Way.") For the young working mother, this could mean, for example, keeping a lid on her temper at work or at home (no matter how justified it may be to lose her temper).

Part of this process means that this young woman has to let go of her desire to be someone else. Because, in reality, she might be lousy at the type of work that Mother Teresa did. But, just to underline this point, Mother Teresa might have been lousy at the work that this working mother is doing!

Saint Francis de Sales, the sixteenth-century bishop of Geneva, touched on this idea in his book *The Introduction to the Devout Life*, when he reflected on the ways that people from different walks of life experience the transcendent.

> When God the Creator made all things, He commanded the plants to bring forth fruit according to its own kind. He has likewise commanded Christians, who are the living plants of his Church, to bring forth the fruits of devotion…in accord with their characters, their stations and their callings…. Therefore, in whatever situations we happen to be, we can and we must aspire to the life of perfection.

Thomas Merton took this one step further. He believed that the person engaged in the "active" life, that is, the laborer or parent or student or caregiver, could lead lives that were in fact more holy, more devout, and more sanctified than those of "professionally religious" people, like the cloistered monk or nun. Merton proposes this in a posthumously published book, *The Inner Experience*, in an essay entitled "Kinds of Contemplation."

> There are many Christians who serve God with great purity of soul and perfect self-sacrifice in the active life….They

know how to find God by devoting themselves to Him in self-sacrificing labors in which they are able to remain in His presence all day long....They lead lives of great simplicity in which they do not need to rise above the ordinary levels of vocal and affective prayer. Without realizing it, their extremely simple prayer is, for them, so deep and interior that it brings them to the threshold of contemplation. Such Christians...may reach a higher degree of sanctity than other who have been apparently favored with a deeper inner life.

Merton calls these men and women "hidden contemplatives" who enjoy a kind of "masked contemplation." Their ability to do so hinges on their willingness to find God not by trying to be cloistered monks, but by discovering the divine spark in their own busy lives.

God's invitation to live out our individual vocations is part of what makes the world so marvelously rich. "How gloriously different are the saints!" wrote the English writer C. S. Lewis. The problem comes when we begin to believe that we have to be someone *else* to be holy. We use someone else's map to heaven when God has already planted in our soul all the directions we need. In that way, we ignore our own call to sanctity. When admirers used to visit Calcutta to see Mother Teresa, she would tell many of them, "Find your own Calcutta." In other words, bloom where you are planted. Discover sanctity in your own life.

This is not to say that we aren't called to emulate the saints or, more to the point, Jesus. Reading the Gospels and the lives of the saints are terrific ways of discovering new paths to holiness. That is part of the discovery process that Merton speaks of: finding yourself within God's conception of yourself. Through prayer and conversation and reading, the working mother gradually finds herself, thanks to God's grace, growing closer to the person she is meant to be. But she is not meant to become Mother Teresa. She is meant to become herself.

As the Jesuit poet Gerard Manley Hopkins wrote in his poem "As Kingfishers Catch Fire":

> for Christ plays in ten thousand places,
> Lovely in limbs, and lovely in eyes not his...

In other words, in your eyes and your limbs.

At the heart of this is accepting who you are before God. "For it was you who formed my inward parts; you knit me together in my mother's womb," in the words of Psalm 139. "I praise you, for I am fearfully and wonderfully made" (13–14). The beginning of sanctity is loving yourself as a creation of God. And that means *all* of yourself, even the parts that you wish weren't there, the parts that you wish God hadn't made, the parts that you lament. God loves us like a parent loves a child—often more for the parts of the child that are weaker or where the child struggles or falters. More often than not, those very weaknesses are the most important paths to holiness, because they remind you of your reliance on God.

"So, I will boast all the more gladly of my weaknesses," wrote Saint Paul, "so that the power of Christ may dwell in me. Therefore I am content with weaknesses, insults, hardships, persecutions, and calamities for the sake of Christ; for whenever I am weak, then I am strong" (2 Cor 12:9–10).

The notion that everyone is called to be a saint has profound implications for daily life. An acceptance of what the Second Vatican Council called the "universal call to holiness" can imbue even the quietest moments of one's life with a special grace. In a beautiful essay called "Sacraments," the American writer Andre Dubus reflects on encountering the holy in his daily life. The author, who died in 1998, had lost the use of both of his legs in an accident that occurred when he was a middle-aged man. One dark night he was standing by the side of a highway, helping a person whose car had broken down, when he was struck by another automobile.

In his essay, Dubus, a devout Catholic, describes the laborious process of making sandwiches for his young daughters to carry with them to school. As he maneuvers his large, bulky wheelchair around his cramped kitchen, as he reaches for the utensils, as he tries to open cabinet doors from his awkward position, and as he cuts the sandwiches, he realizes what he is doing for his children.

> Each moment is a sacrament, this holding of plastic bags, of knives, of bread, of cutting board, this pushing of the chair, this spreading of mustard on bread, this trimming of liverwurst, of ham. All sacraments…

And he grasps the need for an awareness of this reality.

> If I remember it, then I feel it, too.

The universal call to holiness is an invitation to be ourselves. It's also an invitation to remember the sacramentality of everyday life and to realize the great goal that God has set for us: *sanctity*. It is what the saints came to realize, sometimes all at once, sometimes over the course of many years, whether they were born in first-century Palestine like Peter or in twentieth-century America like Dorothy Day. Whether they lived in a quiet cloistered monastery like Thérèse of Lisieux, or in the grand papal palace like Pope John XXIII. Whether they wrote rafts of books like Thomas Merton or Henri Nouwen, or left us with only a handful of their words, like Bernadette Soubirous. Whether they worked alongside the poorest of the poor in Calcutta like Mother Teresa, or with the plague victims in Rome like Aloysius Gonzaga.

Perhaps more to the point, the call to holiness comes whether we work in a corporate office in midtown Manhattan or as a housewife in a small house in Iowa. Whether we are caring for a sick child late at night or preparing a church dinner for hundreds of homeless men and women. Whether we are listening to a friend tell her problems over a cup of coffee or slogging late hours at work in order to help put our children through school. Whether we are patiently spending long hours listening to people in the confessional in a small church, or spending long hours memorizing our lines for a small part in a big Broadway show. Whether we are rich or poor, young or old, man or woman, straight or gay: all of us are called to our own brand of personal holiness.

This brief book has been a meditation on Thomas Merton's idea of the true self. It's about how discovering who we are before God and letting God love that person is an underlying goal of the spiritual life. And it's about how becoming that person can bring us a feeling of union with God and a sense of peace in our lives.

But the book is about something else, too. It's about becoming a saint. Because, in the end, the call to be the true self is an invitation to sanctity. It is a call that transformed the lives of the saints into gifts to the One who loved them into being. The invitation to holiness is a lifelong call to draw closer to God, who wants nothing more than to encounter us as the persons we are, our true selves, and as the saints we are meant to be.

For Further Reading

T
hanks to his many admirers, as well as the man himself, there is no lack of resources about the life and writings of Thomas Merton. Let me recommend a few of my favorites.

Michael Mott's comprehensive biography, *The Seven Mountains of Thomas Merton*, is superb. It's very long, but very worth the effort. He is especially good on the influences in Merton's early life. So is Monica Furlong's *Merton*.

Best of all for understanding Merton's spirituality is M. Basil Pennington's beautiful book *Thomas Merton: Brother Monk*, which uses the idea of "freedom" as the governing spiritual principle in Merton's life. Father Pennington himself was a Trappist monk, which gave him excellent insight into Merton's spiritual life. Interestingly, Pennington offers a mild critique of Michael Mott's book, saying that the book doesn't fully describe the "daily life" that Merton led as a Trappist. Pennington's book provides a good foundation for an understanding of this aspect of Merton's world. I would say that if you wanted to understand Merton, reading those two books—Michael Mott's and Basil Pennington's—would get you most of the way there. Father Pennington, as a matter of fact, published a book called *True Self/False Self*, which came highly recommended, but which I intentionally did not read, since I did not want to be guilty of copying anything he had written. If there are any similarities between our two books, they are both unintentional and providential.

Henri Nouwen wrote a lovely book of essays on Merton entitled *Encounters with Merton*. Also though they have less to do with Merton's spirituality, I've always enjoyed *The Man in the Sycamore Tree*, a personal meditation on Merton by his longtime friend Edward Rice; as well as *The Hermitage Journals*, by John Howard Griffin, the journal of Griffin's time at Gethsemani. (Griffin, the author of *Black Like Me*, was Merton's first choice for his official biographer, but died before he could finish his work. The job then passed to Michael Mott.)

Though not specifically about the true self, Richard Rohr's book *Adam's Return* includes an excellent discussion about how men in particular have a difficult time embracing the true self.

As for Merton's own works, if you haven't already read *The Seven Storey Mountain*, perhaps it's time you should! Though it is one of my favorite books, there are some readers who say they don't enjoy it (too long, too self-centered, too triumphalistic about Catholicism, they say). I think it's important to accept it for what it is: the story of a conversion written by a bright, strong-willed young man.

In many ways, for me, *The Sign of Jonas* is a more enjoyable book, written after some of Merton's starry-eyed idealism has worn off. I find it his warmest and most personal book. If you are completely dedicated to learning all you can about Merton, you can now read all of his unabridged journals, volumes one through seven, under the titles *Run to the Mountain* (edited by Patrick Hart), *Entering the Silence* (edited by Jonathan Montaldo), *The Search for Solitude* (edited by Lawrence S. Cunningham), *Turning Toward the World* (edited by Victor Kramer), *Dancing in the Water of Life* (edited by Robert E. Daggy), *Learning to Love* (edited by Christine M. Bohlen), and *The Other Side of the Mountain* (edited by Patrick Hart).

For readers with less time, you might start off with *The Secular Journal*, which covers Merton's time before his entrance to Gethsemani, as well as *The Intimate Merton: His Life from His Journals* (edited by Jonathan Montaldo and Patrick Hart), a fine abridged collection of all of his journals.

As for his books on meditation, my favorites are *No Man is an Island* and, of course, *New Seeds of Contemplation*, where he speaks in detail about the idea of the "true self." Of course, Thomas Merton does a much better job with it than I ever could!

Finally, two excellent single-volume anthologies of Merton's own writings are *Thomas Merton: Spiritual Master* (edited by Lawrence S. Cunningham), and *I Have Seen What I Was Looking For* (edited by M. Basil Pennington).

If you're interested in reading something by Henri Nouwen, you could start with *The Genesee Diary: Report from a Trappist Monastery* and *The Return of the Prodigal Son*. Other popular Nouwen titles are *The Life of the Beloved* and *Adam: God's Beloved*. An excellent biography to begin with is *Wounded Prophet: A Portrait of Henri J.M. Nouwen*, by Michael Ford. A fine book for understanding Nouwen's own spiritual journey is *God's Beloved: A Spiritual Biography of Henri Nouwen*, by

Michael O'Laughlin. The Henri Nouwen Society also maintains a website (www.henrinouwen.org), upon which I drew for my brief description of Nouwen's life.

For an excellent treatment of the idea of the "self-knowledge" of Jesus, you can turn to *Consider Jesus*, by Elizabeth Johnson, CSJ, perhaps the best short introduction to "Christology" today, and Albert Nolan's fascinating and entirely accessible *Jesus Before Christianity*, which focuses on his life in first-century Palestine.

Finally, for a terrific introduction to the variety of ways in which the saints became holy, *All Saints*, by Robert Ellsberg, is a marvelous compendium of short biographies of the saints, both traditional and nontraditional. Ellsberg's next book, *The Saints' Guide to Happiness*, draws lessons from the lives of the saints, showing how being one's "true self" can ultimately lead to a happy life. Both books will remind you that we are all called to be, in the words of Blessed Pope John XXIII, "holy in a different way."

Acknowledgments

T his small book proved to be a big project, one that could only have been completed with the help of many people.

Many thanks, first of all, to Father Raymond M. Rafferty of Corpus Christi Church, the International Thomas Merton Society, the Henri Nouwen Society, and the Center for Spiritual Development of the Archdiocese of New York, for inviting me to give the lecture from which this book eventually grew. Before the lecture began, Father Rafferty escorted me into a little parlor in the church's rectory, and said I could wait there for a few minutes. As he closed the door, he mentioned that it was the very room where Merton first asked to become a Catholic. It was a wonderful moment for me.

There were a number of experts who read this book as it neared completion and generously offered advice, comments, and corrections. I am exceedingly grateful to Jonathan Montaldo, the former director of the Thomas Merton Center and co-editor of *The Intimate Merton*; Michael O'Laughlin, author of *God's Beloved: A Spiritual Biography of Henri Nouwen*; Michael Ford, author of *Wounded Prophet: A Portrait of Henri J.M. Nouwen*; Sue Mosteller, CSJ, of the Henri Nouwen Center; and Daniel J. Harrington, SJ, professor of New Testament at the

Weston Jesuit School of Theology. Their expertise and assistance were invaluable. As the book neared completion, William A. Barry, SJ, reviewed the manuscript and provided a helpful commentary that helped to deepen my discussion of several topics, particularly the chapter on the self-knowledge of Jesus.

Paul McMahon of Paulist Books invited me to write this book, and so I am grateful to him, as I am to Kevin Carrizo di Camillo, also of Paulist, for his continuing support and enthusiasm. I am also thankful to John Jones for his advice on this project. Damien O'Connell, SJ, my spiritual director, was of great help with this book, as he is with everything in my life. And I thank David I. Donovan, SJ, my spiritual director in the Jesuit novitiate, for his help in my journey toward self-discovery and self-awareness all those years ago. His sudden death in 2005 left many of his friends feeling bereft, but also confident that they had a new friend in heaven praying for them. This little book is dedicated to him.

My Jesuit faith-sharing group, Chris Derby, SJ, Matt Cassidy, SJ, Chris Devron, SJ, and Jim McDermott, SJ, is wonderfully supportive and challenging, and I am very grateful for them. George Williams, SJ, Steve Katsouros, SJ, and Bob Reiser, SJ, were also great supports during the time of writing this book. Thanks also to Dave Gibson, Tim Reidy, Grant Gallicho, Bill McGarvey, Robert Ellsberg, Ron Hansen, Tom Beaudoin, and Jeremy Langford for their encouragement about writing in general and their friendship.

Thanks to Thomas J. Reese, SJ, editor of *America* magazine, where I was also working when I wrote this book. During his time at the magazine, he taught me a great deal about being who you are, and being the person God called you to be.

During the writing of this book, I was also helping an acting company with a play called *The Last Days of Judas*

Iscariot, and so for their questions, their curiosity, and their companionship, I want to thank the members of that production with the LAByrinth Theater Company, especially Stephen Adly Guirgis, Sam Rockwell, Phil Hoffman, and John Ortiz. They helped me think about Jesus from a fresh perspective and meditate on his self-knowledge in surprising new ways.

Finally, since I have drawn extensively on their scholarship for my own research, prayer, and inspiration over many years, I would like to thank Michael Mott, Monica Furlong, John Howard Griffin, M. Basil Pennington, OCSO, Jonathan Montaldo, Patrick Hart, OCSO, Edward Rice, Paul Pearson, William Shannon, James Forest, and Paul Wilkes for their marvelous work on Thomas Merton.

I would also like to thank the following for their kind permission to allow me use of their material:

Cover photograph of Thomas Merton by John Howard Griffin. Used with permission of the Merton Legacy Trust and the Griffin Estate.

Cover photograph of Henri J. M. Nouwen by Peter K. Weiskel. Used by Permission of the Henri Nouwen Society and Peter K. Weiskel.

Cover photograph of Mother Teresa courtesy of W. P. Wittman, Limited, 1706 Missenden Cres., Mississauga, Ontario, Canada, L5J 2T4. www.wpwittman.com. Used by permission.

Excerpts from *The Seven Storey Mountain* © 1948; *New Seeds of Contemplation* © 1961; *No Man Is an Island* © 1955; *Conjectures of a Guilty Bystander* © 1966; and *The Secular Journal of Thomas Merton* © 1959—all reprinted by permission of The Trustees of the Merton Legacy Trust and The Abbey of Gethsemani. Used with permission of the Merton Legacy Trust.

Excerpt from *The Last Days of Judas Iscariot* by Stephen Adly Guirgis © 2005 by Stephen Adly Guirgis. Used by permission of the playwright.

"As Kingfishers Catch Fire" by Gerard Manley Hopkins from *The Poems of Gerard Manley Hopkins* © 1970. Used by permission of Oxford University Press on behalf of the British Province of the Society of Jesus. www.oup.com.

About the Author

The Rev. James Martin, SJ, is a Jesuit priest and associate editor of *America*, a national Catholic magazine. A graduate of the University of Pennsylvania's Wharton School of Business, he worked for six years in corporate finance before entering the Society of Jesus in 1988. During his Jesuit training he worked in a hospice for the sick and dying in Kingston, Jamaica; with street-gang members in Chicago; as a prison chaplain in Boston; and for two years with East African refugees in Nairobi, Kenya. After completing his philosophy and theology studies, he was ordained a priest in 1999.

Father Martin's writing has appeared in a variety of newspapers and magazines, both in the United States and abroad, and he is a frequent commentator in the media on religion and spirituality. He is the author and editor of a number of books, including his memoirs *In Good Company: The Fast Track from the Corporate World to Poverty, Chastity and Obedience* (Sheed & Ward) and *This Our Exile: A Spiritual Journey with the Refugees of East Africa* (Orbis). His most recent book is *My Life with the Saints* (Loyola).